Poverty first hand

Poor people speak for themselves

Peter Beresford • David Green • Ruth Lister • Kirsty Woodard

LEARNING
RESOURCES
CENTRE

HAVERING
COLLEGE

CPAG • 94 WHITE LION STREET • LONDON N1 9PF

CPAG promotes action for the relief, directly or indirectly, of poverty among children and families with children. We work to ensure that those on low incomes get their full entitlements to welfare benefits. In our campaigning and information work we seek to improve benefits and policies for low income families, in order to eradicate the injustice of poverty. If you are not already supporting us, please consider making a donation, or ask for details of our membership schemes and publications.

Poverty Publication 99

Published by CPAG
94 White Lion Street, London N1 9PF

© CPAG 1999

ISBN 0 946744 89 0

A CIP record for this book is available from the British Library

Design and page-make-up by studio@deviousdesigns.co.uk in memory of Nancy White
Printed by Progressive Printing UK Ltd 01702 524028

ACKNOWLEDGEMENTS

We have many people to thank for helping to make this book and the project on which it is based possible. First we must thank all the groups and people with experience of poverty who took part in the group discussions which are at the heart of the book. It can be very difficult talking about something when for much of the time you are devalued for that experience. We want to thank the many people who took part in the project for sharing their ideas, knowledge and experience with us, for the skills and effort which they put into the project and for their continuing involvement, which has made this book possible.

We also want to express our thanks to all the individuals and organisations who put us in touch with groups. We should also like to thank colleagues who have given us insight and support, particularly Suzy Croft for her help in undertaking some of the group discussions.

Last, but not least, we want to thank Brunel University and the Joseph Rowntree Charitable Trust for the financial support which they gave to this project.and the commitment which they made to it. It is always difficult to get funding to take forward new and controversial ideas. This work was no exception. Without their help, neither the book nor project would have been possible.

Peter Beresford, Brunel University and Open Services Project;
David Green, University of West of England;
Ruth Lister, Loughborough University;
Kirsty Woodward, Age Concern.

Political empowerment of poor people.
People must organise for collective action to influence
the circumstances and decisions affecting their lives.
To advance their interests, their voices must be heard
in the corridors of power.

(United Nations Development Programme, 1997, p94)

CONTENTS

FOREWORD

Poverty First Hand is an important and powerful book. At a time when the debate on poverty (and how to end it) is at a crucial stage, the discussion needs to be as inclusive and informed as possible. The people who have most to contribute are those who experience the problem at first hand. This book is a response to the fact that people living in poverty are rarely listened to and rarely have an opportunity for their voices to be heard.

When we talk about poverty we sometimes need to remind ourselves (particularly when we claim to speak on behalf of people living in poverty) that we are talking about real people. We need to move on from abstract concepts, theories and 'case studies'. This book *is* about real people – about their experiences, but also their thoughts, opinions and concerns.

Their is no shortage of research about poverty and social exclusion. Collecting the facts and evidence is a crucial part in the process of change – we need to engage the politicians and to win the arguments. But there is a danger that people's lives are distilled to numbers on a page – the larger and more daunting the statistics become, the more we become desensitised and detached. Rarely do those who are poor get to present their experience; rarely are their arguments discussed.

When the pressure groups, academics and politicians talk about 'poverty' and 'the poor', we may sometimes be talking about 'us', but more often we are talking about 'them'. The poor are spectators – they may not even recognise that the debate is about them.

In this book people living in poverty are encouraged to communicate directly, without their words being 'analysed', filtered or interpreted. What is said does not always make for comfortable reading – stereotypes and myths are challenged and the language is sometime strong.

From the start the authors recognised that poverty can be isolating. It was not sufficient to parachute into communities and invite people to a meeting. New methods and processes needed to be adopted to ensure that there was genuine participation. Time and energy were spent reaching people living in poverty and ensuring that people were able to speak for themselves. The process was time-consuming. Care was taken to go back to the people that took part to ensure that they agreed with what was being presented as their voice. Although the discussions in this book took place before the election of the present Labour Government, the contributions remain as important and relevant to the issues today. This book helps take the debate forward.

For anyone involved in the poverty debate, this is an exciting time. The Prime Minister, Tony Blair, made a pledge (in March 1999) to end child poverty within a generation. While the commitment should be applauded, the challenge for organisations like CPAG is to ensure that the promise is kept. There have been some promising first steps, but the record so far has not been consistent. We still hear Ministers talking about 'dependency'. In an exclusive in the Daily Mail in February 1999, Tony Blair said that he would end 'the something for nothing welfare state'.

Ending poverty will not be easy – but it can be done. Radical measures are necessary, we need new ideas. Poverty will continue to exist until the people who experience it daily are fully involved – they must be participants and not just spectators. This book throws down a challenge to organisations like CPAG – we must never take for granted that we have all the answers, we should remember who we claim to act for. People living in poverty must be able to speak – but we must also be willing to listen.

Martin Barnes, Director, Child Poverty Action Group.

INTRODUCTION

There is growing political and public debate about poverty and its relation with crime, welfare 'dependency' social breakdown and changes in family patterns, particularly the increase in the number of lone parents. People on low income and with first hand experience of poverty have generally had little voice in this discussion, except to illustrate it. Little has been heard about their ideas about or theories of poverty; the efforts they make both to challenge poverty and to struggle against its damaging effects; or their proposals for combatting poverty.

The purpose of this book is to address this gap by providing an opportunity for people with experience of poverty to say what *they* think about poverty. It aims to enable them to engage in the debate and put forward their own views, analysis, ideas and proposals about poverty, to inform discussion and offer a greater balance by including *all* key stakeholders. It seeks to bring together in an accessible way what people with experience of poverty have to say in their own words and under their own control. In doing this, its goal is both to build on the growing body of work which describes the effects of poverty, using the words of those with experience of it and to take forward a new approach which is committed to involving poor people themselves as fully as possible in anti-poverty discussion and action. We see the book as one step in a process of supporting people with experience of poverty to have their own debates and to be equal members of mainstream debates about poverty.

THE BACKGROUND TO THE BOOK

The book is based on a two year participatory research project supported by the Joseph Rowntree Charitable Trust and Brunel University. The focus of the project follows from an earlier meeting that two of us organised, which brought together people with experience of poverty and anti-poverty professionals, to talk about the involvement of poor people in anti-poverty action. The book draws on a series of group discussions with a wide range of poor people in Britain, including, for example, young people, lone parents, older people, women, disabled people, young offenders, parents with small children, homeless and unemployed people. We have also tried to ensure the inclusion of people facing discrimination on grounds of 'race', gender, age, disability and sexual orientation. The group discussions were carried out between January 1994 and June 1995.

We spoke with people in many parts of the country. Poverty can be an isolating experience. We worked hard to reach people, using leaflets, newsletters, word of mouth, our own networks and those of other organisations. Many of the people who took part were involved in groups, including support, self-help, community, campaigning and self-advocacy groups. (see Appendix 2 for details of the groups) While the participants are not presented as representative of all people with experience of poverty, they nonetheless offer the views of a wide range of poor people. The project is a qualitative rather than quantitative study, although where there are significant differences in what individuals or groups say, these are highlighted.

In the past, when poor people have been asked about poverty, it has generally been to ask them what it is like to be poor. This book takes poor people's experience as its starting point to explore with them their thoughts about poverty much more broadly. It rests on the increasingly widespread belief that poor people, like other oppressed groups, have a right to speak for themselves; that it is important to ask them what they think and that discussions and developments which include people's first hand views are likely to be more effective and make more progress than those which don't.

The perspective poor people have on poverty is genuinely new and exciting, because they have so far had so few chances to express their views. Now is a particularly good time to hear them. There is a new interest in people speaking for themselves which cuts across political, ideological and professional divides. There is new enthusiasm for the grassroots activities of poor people. Initiatives which seek to involve poor people are beginning to blossom, as can be seen from the examples in the first part of the book. This approach is based on a new participatory process which brings with it a changed relationship between anti-poverty professionals and poor people themselves. In research, this means a different *process* which seeks to involve people with experience of poverty as fully as possible. This approach also makes it possible to explore new ground, like poor people's own interpretations of poverty and proposals for change, as well as offering a check and new insights on earlier findings. It is our belief that the inclusion of poor people heralds a vital new stage in anti-poverty discussions, campaigns and policy. We hope this book may play a part in informing and influencing these; both by conveying what poor people actually say and by extending the principle and process of researching and faithfully reproducing their views and ideas in a participatory and emancipatory way.

When this project was carried out, a Conservative government was in power. Now for the first time for 18 years a Labour government is in office. This administration embraces new ideas and raises new issues. At the same time, its approach to welfare reform has raised concerns among anti-poverty and service users' organisations. But its emphasis on a new form of politics, embracing citizen juries, focus groups, referendums and other new forms of local representation, opens up possibilities of involving and including people who are poor. The Government's establishment of a Social Exclusion Unit also offers a new focus for anti-poverty policy and action. Its acknowledgement that poverty is a problem to be tackled by government offers a degree of hope for the future. The advent of this new political era makes it even more important to listen to what poor people themselves have to say.

THE AUTHORS

The project on which this book is based was jointly supervised by Peter Beresford and Ruth Lister. Kirsty Woodard was the first project worker and she was succeeded by David Green.

In recent years there has been some questioning of the idea of neutral, and value-free social science and recognition that the researcher's particular standpoint may affect the design, process and objectives of research and how s/he interprets the data.[1]

The four of us have very different backgrounds and experiences, but issues of poverty and participation are in different ways important in all of them. Three of us have direct experience of poverty. David Green's family lived on benefits when he was in his teens. From the age of six until her teens, Kirsty Woodard lived in a family of eight reliant on one low wage. Peter Beresford lived on benefits for more than eight years, bringing up a family with his partner. Ruth Lister worked for the Child Poverty Action Group for 16 years.

All of us in have been concerned with supporting people to secure their rights and speak for themselves. David Green formerly advocated for people with mental distress and Kirsty Woodard is now an advocacy officer working with older people. Peter Beresford is actively involved in a self-advocacy organisation of recipients of mental health services, Survivors Speak Out. The activities of Child Poverty Action Group, with which Ruth Lister worked, include 'promoting action for the relief of poverty among children and families', ensuring that 'those on low income get their full entitlement to welfare benefits' and providing advice for welfare rights workers locally.

We believe that our different backgrounds and experience have helped us to recognise both the differences between professional and first hand perspectives on poverty and also the contributions which each has to make. We have also come to appreciate what these different perspectives can learn and gain from each other. Equally, each of us has learned from the others. We feel we have benefited from this cooperation. We hope that the approach this book offers will be equally positive and helpful for other people; both those with direct experience of poverty and those working to support them and in challenging poverty.

We don't have one narrow view about poverty and we would not wish to impose such a view on others. At the same time we are aware that the involvement of people on the receiving end of public policy in discussions and policy development, can be challenging and uncomfortable for traditional stakeholders. Strong feelings and emotions can be generated. These need to be recognised, acknowledged, respected and addressed. In this book we seek to challenge longstanding exclusions, not to encourage new ones. Our aim is to help develop an *inclusive* debate on poverty where the knowledge, experience and contributions of different groups and interests are equally valued. If a dent is to be made on a problem as intractable as poverty, then values of inclusion, participation and cooperation are at a premium. They are the values with which we have sought to underpin this book.

THE STRUCTURE OF THE BOOK

The book is divided into three parts. The first part sets in context the involvement of people with experience of poverty. It begins by examining existing approaches to poverty discussions and developments, looking at who is involved, the definition of poverty, language and images associated with poverty and the causes and solutions which are identified. The second chapter explores the issue of the involvement of poor people themselves; the implications this has for poverty debates and developments, and existing initiatives to involve people with experience of poverty. It describes some of the exciting new developments that are taking place to involve and include people with experience of poverty in anti-poverty discussions and action. There is also a brief discussion of the project on which this book is based, which examines the philosophy underpinning it and the methods used to carry it out.

The second part of the book reports the views of people with experience of poverty themselves. These chapters, Chapters 3 to 7, make up the main part of the book. They are based on what people said in the project. Unusually for books about poverty, it is their words which make up most of the text. Instead of providing our own analysis, we have tried to give priority to people's *own* views and understandings, letting them speak for themselves. Each of these chapters concludes with a brief summary of what participants have said.

Chapter 3 looks at what people with experience of poverty have to say about the definition of poverty, including their views on dominant definitions and their own implicit and explicit definitions. Chapter 4, focuses on what they see as the causes of poverty. Chapter 5 offers their views on the effects of poverty. Chapter 6 explores their analysis of the images and language of poverty, reflected in current media and political representations of poverty; what they think of current poverty imagery, including, for example, that of lone parents and delinquency and ideas of 'the underclass' and 'dependency'. Chapter 7 looks at participants' proposals for action on poverty ; what role they see for people with experience of poverty in anti-poverty action and discussions at local and national levels and their own experience of being involved.

The third and final part of the book looks to the future. Chapter 8 pulls together some of the issues raised in the project, offers some of the authors' thoughts about them and explores the implications for the future of poverty debates and anti-poverty action. This is followed by three Appendices offering readers additional information about the project on which the book is based. The first Appendix details the method and methodology of the research project; setting out in full how it was carried out and the philosophy which underpinned it. The second gives details of the groups which took part, describing who they are and their composition. The third

Appendix provides a copy of the semi-structured schedule used in group discussion. Next, readers will find details of notes and references offered in the text. Finally there is a short bibliography of material which readers might find helpful in exploring further some of the issues raised in the book.

Poverty is a complex subject. We have tried not to assume knowledge on the part of readers. At the same time this is not another introductory textbook on poverty. Some readers may be familiar with the arguments we report when we set the scene or feel that they have been oversimplified. If this happens, we suggest they move on past familiar ground. The important part of the book is where people with experience of poverty speak for themselves. It is to their words the reader should give priority.

NOTES

1 H Roberts (editor), *Doing Feminist Research*, Routledge and Kegan Paul, 1981; P Reason and J Rowan (editors), *Human Inquiry: A source book of new paradigm research,* John Wiley, 1981: Disability, Handicap and Society, Special Issue, Vol 7, No 2, 1992; M Rioux and M Bach (editors), *Disability is not Measles: New research paradigms in disability,* L'Institut Roeher, 1994.

Part One

SETTING THE SCENE

INTRODUCTION

The facts about the scale of inequality in Britain still fail to ignite a popular outcry ... But there is an equal and telling silence at the bottom.

(Will Hutton, 1995)[1]

People in poverty should be listened to and heard ... More of the money raised to combat poverty should go to poor people themselves so they can set up and run their own organisations and projects.

(Poor people talking in: UK Coalition Against Poverty, Participation Sub-Group, 1997)[2]

These comments take us to the heart of why a new debate about poverty in the UK is developing. The two questions which Will Hutton's quotation begs: why *isn't* there a public outcry about inequality? and why *aren't* poor people's voices to be heard?, are essential starting points for this book. In this section, we set the scene for the book. We look at current debates and developments about poverty and their relationship with poor people. This leads on to an examination of two different discussions about poverty. One has been played out in parliamentary chambers and lobbies, editorial offices, seminar rooms and campaign headquarters. The other is rooted in the lives of people with experience of poverty themselves, in their day-to-day struggles, understanding and achievements. There are overlaps between the two discussions. Neither is monolithic. What most distinguishes them is who takes part. By exploring them both, it may be possible to discover an explanation for the situation which Will Hutton reports.

NOTES

1 W Hutton, Why the Poor Remain Silent, *Guardian*, 13 February 1995.
2 UK Coalition Against Poverty, Participation Sub-Group, *Poverty and Participation: Learnings from a September 1996 workshop bringing together people living in poverty throughout the UK*, UK Coalition Against Poverty, 1997.

Poverty at Second Hand: Conventional approaches to the analysis and politics of poverty

THE KEY AGENTS INVOLVED IN SHAPING DOMINANT POVERTY DEBATES

For most people social problems are facts of life. But they are also the product of the human agencies and institutions involved in shaping and interpreting them. This is as true for poverty as it is for other social problems. Four key agents have shaped dominant debates and developments about poverty. These are academics, the poverty lobby, politicians and the media.

They all have their different histories, interests, objectives and ideologies. None of them is homogeneous or monolithic. There are variations of view and approach within each. There are also significant similarities and overlaps between them; for example, in perspectives and personnel. Academics are recruited as political advisers and members of official committees. Poverty lobbyists develop close political links with or become politicians themselves. Some politicians and academics are involved in pressure groups and pressure group leaders sometimes become academics. None of these agents exists in isolation. All are interrelated. All play a part in the formation of poverty and the way different publics understand it. They operate closely together. There is both conflict and cooperation. They also interact with broader economic and geopolitical forces.

ACADEMICS

While there are poverty academics of all political colours, the dominant academic tradition in the UK is a left-of-centre social administration one. It has been closely associated with state welfare and concerned with the accumulation of expert evidence about poverty as a basis for analysis and action. The 'rediscovery of poverty' in the 1960s was due to this work and academics have continued to provide important evidence about poverty and its effects. However, it has also tended to be pre-occupied with issues of definition and measurement and to be more descriptive than theoretical.[1] More recently, though, there is beginning to emerge a more theoretical approach to understanding poverty.[2]

POVERTY LOBBY

The UK poverty lobby embraces two traditions. The first is that of specific anti-poverty pressure groups, campaigning charities which grew out of the 1960s academic 'rediscovery of poverty', like the Child Poverty Action Group, Disablement Income Group and later the Low Pay Unit. Second, there are the more service and project oriented charities, like, Barnardos, Save the Children Fund, The Children's Society and Family Welfare Association, which in recent years have become increasingly involved in anti-poverty campaigning work. As Alcock notes, the poverty lobby has incorporated 'an increasingly wide range of specialist groups and umbrella organisations.'[3] The organisations associated with the poverty lobby are national, some with local groups and branches. It operates in a broader context of anti-poverty action from churches, trade unions and local voluntary and community organisations and campaigns. In recent years it has been further extended by cooperation and collaboration between pressure groups, for example, the Social Security Consortium which brings together a wide range of poverty lobby groups together with the local authority associations. Organisations like CPAG were set up to meet a very different situation to that which they have subsequently encountered. Established to put pressure on left-of-centre Labour regimes, they have since had to respond to a different challenge and deal with successive Conservative administrations, with fundamentally different values and objectives. Suzanne Macgregor offers a clear expression of the conventional view of such pressure groups.

> (They) act as watchdogs on the activities of Governments on behalf of their clients or members. They remind Governments of their responsibilities and their promises , comment on developments in policy and practice and propose solutions.[4]

The poverty lobby has been predominantly *promotional* in nature; that is promoting issues for, but not by, poor people. Its membership and staff are largely non-poor, although CPAG, for example, has made some effort to involve poor people in its local branches.[5] While the poverty lobby and indeed academics, include people with experience of poverty, they are more likely to be involved in a professional capacity than on the basis of that experience. The poverty lobby has generally adopted a top-down, rather than bottom-up approach to its activities. Lobbying is mainly carried out by anti-poverty professionals. For example, Whitehall 'mandarins' are thought to be most effectively approached by mandarin-like figures. In their study of anti-poverty pressure groups, Whiteley and Winyard concluded:

> Apart from the problems of organising the poor into representative groups, those setting up the groups did not believe in the need for a large membership given that the aim was to influence elite opinion ... As far as group strategies are concerned, it might be argued that a Fabian strategy would be a focused 'insider' strategy ... groups obviously sought to be acceptable to the elite civil servants and politicians in Whitehall.[6]

POLITICIANS

The fundamental differences between the traditional political right and left have profound implications for poverty, with the right's commitment to individual freedom and the private market and the left's to social justice, state intervention and equality. But for the first 25 years of the British welfare state, under what is known as 'the post-war settlement', these differences were essentially put on hold, as Conservative governments maintained the essential principles of the welfare state, even if their degree of commitment to it varied. This ended during the 1970s with major economic changes and the arrival of right wing Conservative governments which challenged the values and assumption underlying the welfare state. This meant a dramatic change in the political context of poverty during the 1980s, reflected also in New Labour policies in the 1990s. We will return to the political context later in the chapter.

THE MEDIA

The media both reflect and help create political agendas on poverty. They are involved in shaping policy as well as transmitting and presenting it. They are themselves politically positioned and in the case of print media, this is predominantly and overtly right-of-centre. Nor does poverty generally figure high in prevailing news values, except where poor people come in for attack. One former social services correspondent, Peter Hildrew wrote:

> Poverty may be a running phenomenon of our times, but it is not a news story and it can be pretty flat. Few in the media see it as their job to alter the condition of the poor; they will only pay attention when something quite unusual is happening. Their craft lies rather in knowing how to exploit a story once it starts running, when to pick it up and when to let it drop.[7]

The media, like the other agents involved in the social construction of poverty, largely reflect non-poor voices. This has important implications for their own understandings of poverty, which cut across conventional political and ideological divisions. Thus Melanie Phillips wrote candidly in the left-of-centre Guardian:

> I would regard it as a terrible mark of failure to claim unemployment benefit. Journalists can always find work. It would mean that I had no initiative to find a job. I would feel it wrong not to work, even clerical or something ... Perhaps I do consciously look on people who are unemployed in a more critical way than I think I do... Journalists do think that other people can get work. Most are middle class ... the whole issue of social services is alien to them. If they have problems they use middle-class solutions. The Welfare State is outside the experience of most journalists.[8]

It is not possible here to offer a detailed media analysis, but the overall picture seems to be of a press response which generally runs on traditional political lines. While there are exceptions, like, for example, the Daily Mail story: 'Don't bash the benefit claimants, says report'[9] the punitive approach continues in the tabloids,[10] with a more sympathetic approach on the whole in left of centre broadsheets. Although this runs the risk of treating poor people as victims, there are beginning to be some signs of reporting what people in poverty themselves are saying[11] and of including them in radio and TV news discussions about poverty.

THE POLITICS OF CHANGE

As we have already seen, however, each of the different agents described above as well as having its own identity is part of an overall process of social problem and policy formation. This raises the question of how they relate to each other in debates and developments around poverty. The expected division of labour might be that:

- academics do research and develop theories
- pressure groups publicise the evidence and pressurise governments and politicians
- politicians decide and make policy
- media influence policy and shape public views of poverty.

But power differences between these constituencies also have an important bearing on what they do and how they work together. Politicians are clearly pivotal in the process, but the role of the media is crucial too. Its importance for other agents, particularly for pressure groups, cannot be overestimated. The media not only shapes public knowledge and understanding of poverty; it is also the crucial conduit through which pressure group messages must be communicated to make an impact. Politicians tend to respond to media stories more than detailed argument. This has much to do with the model of change upon which the dominant anti-poverty discussion has been based. To sum up this model of change has been characterised by:

- an emphasis on a top-down, predominantly parliamentary approach, narrowly based on the idea of experts gathering evidence as a basis for change, backed up by use of the media to influence both politicians and public opinion;
- a tradition of social administration solutions to social problems, the high point of which was the massive expansion of social work and social services in the early 1970s when they were presented as an effective response to poverty;
- significant overlaps of class, culture, networks and experience between the four different agents involved in poverty discussion, with poor people themselves as 'the other'; objects of concern, contempt, hostility or sometimes even fear.

THE MAIN ELEMENTS OF POVERTY DEBATE

The rest of this chapter presents the main elements of these overlapping discussions. There are three issues and areas on which discussions have focused: the definitions, the language and images, and the causes and solutions of poverty.

DEFINITIONS OF POVERTY

The definition of poverty has assumed enormous importance in poverty debates. It is one of the most contentious issues in such discussions. This is perhaps not surprising given how significant and controversial an issue poverty is. This focus should not be seen as merely an ivory tower exercise. We cannot ignore it, instead we need to understand it. It tells us a lot about the nature of both poverty and poverty debates. As Alcock says:

> Disagreements over the definition of poverty run deep and are closely associated with disagreements over both the causes of and the solutions to it. In practice all these issues of definition, measurement, cause and solution are bound up together.
>
> ... Arguably it is the issue of definition which lies at the heart of the task of understanding poverty. We must first know what poverty is before we can identify where and when it is occurring or attempt to measure it; and before we can do anything to alleviate it.[12]

While there are links and overlaps between academic, political, pressure group and media debates, there are also important differences between them in the way they approach the definition of poverty.[13]

• ACADEMIC DEFINITIONS

As Suzanne Macgregor says, 'The academic debate about poverty has been largely about definitions.'[14] Two approaches to the definition of poverty have predominated since this discussion began more than a hundred years ago; *relative* and *absolute* definitions. The academic debate about the concept of poverty 'has focussed primarily on the issue of an absolute versus a relative concept'.[15] This debate has been long and fierce, with many disagreements. Because of this it is helpful to set out these two definitions briefly.

Seebohm Rowntree who began the tradition of absolute definitions at the end of the last century, defined families whose 'total earnings are insufficient to obtain the minimum necessaries for the maintenance of merely physical efficiency as being in primary poverty'. The absolute definition of poverty is based upon the notion of subsistence. Subsistence is the minimum needed to sustain life, and so being below subsistence level is to be experiencing absolute poverty because one does not have enough to live on.[16] By this definition, being poor means not having food to eat, clothes on your back or shelter over your head.

The relative definition grew out of the revulsion of young academics and campaigners in the 1960s against assumptions that the welfare state had put an end to poverty. Peter Townsend, the best known of these, put it in these terms.

> Individuals, families and groups in the population can be said to be in poverty when they lack the resources to obtain the types of diet, participate in the activities and have the living conditions and amenities which are customary...in the societies to which they belong.[17]

Carol and Alan Walker make clear the distinction that is drawn between absolute and relative definitions of poverty.

> Rather than asking whether incomes are sufficient to maintain a pre-determined level of physical efficiency, the relative conception of poverty asks to what extent are the poor able to participate in the lives of the societies in which they live.[18]

Thus one definition is based on the individual's physical state, the other on his or her relation to the society in which they live. The absolute definition is generally regarded as a much narrower, harsher and more basic definition of poverty.

Both approaches to the definition of poverty have been developed and refined over time, so that, for example, more generous subsistence definitions have been introduced. Both have had advocates who have argued their objectivity, for example, Rowntree for an absolute definition and Townsend for a relative one. Both, however, have been shown to rest on value judgements and have major limitations.[19] Neither has commanded consensus. Both have been used as a basis for measuring poverty, but neither has made possible agreement about how it should be measured.

Increasingly, however, social scientists are suggesting that the distinction between absolute and relative poverty is blurred and illusory. It can ultimately be argued that all conceptions of poverty are relative since it is not possible to divorce the determination of even basic physical needs from the conventions and customs of the society in which they have to be met. As Carol and Alan Walker conclude:

> on closer inspection of the arguments... we discover that the real different between contemporary approaches to poverty is not actually between relative versus absolute concepts. Virtually everyone agrees that poverty is a relative phenomenon but the differences lie in the degree of generosity or parsimony built into the definition.[20]

Pete Alcock adds:

> Thus absolute definitions of poverty necessarily involve relative judgements to apply them to any particular society; and relative definitions require some absolute core in order to distinguish them from broader inequalities...In practice most attempts to define and measure poverty do combine both...usually by selecting a poverty standard, expressing it in income terms and then applying it to the income distribution of a particular society in order to reveal the proportion in poverty.[21]

There have long been some commentators within the dominant poverty debate who have been critical of its preoccupation with definition and measurement. Others have tried to create more democratic 'consensual' definitions of poverty by involving the general population in the process of definition, which even if they don't specifically include poor people, don't exclude them.[22] As Pete Alcock reminds us:

> attempts to define poverty as a distinct social phenomenon have been developed in order to create political pressure for recognition of such levels of deprivation as problematic and an acceptance by politicians that something must be done about them. It is this quest which gives the definition of poverty its social meaning, indeed arguably its *only* meaning.[23]

• POVERTY LOBBY DEFINITIONS

The main source of such political pressure in the UK today is the poverty lobby. The activities of the poverty lobby are effectively based on a blurred definition of poverty. While it tends to subscribe to a relative definition, highlighting poor people's exclusion from many activities in society, many of the examples it uses to illustrate poverty are ones which fit an absolute definition. This includes

people going without sufficient food, warmth or basic clothing and
lacking shelter. It has also used measures which are linked with both
definitions. Where absolute poverty was seen by some as a thing of
the past in the 1960s, major economic and political changes since
then, have dramatically altered the situation. The poverty lobby has
provided and drawn on evidence to show increases in poverty based
on both relative and more absolute measures in the 1980s and 1990s.
Organisations like the Child Poverty Action Group have subjected
definitions and measures to critical consideration, as well as using
them as a basis for their campaigning. As Sally Witcher, former
director of the Child Poverty Action Group says of the two different
measures used by government in recent years:

> It would be wrong to assume that the facts will always be believed, or
> even that they should be accepted unchallenged. CPAG certainly
> examines them critically...Yet this does not justify the extent to which
> issues clearly revealed by research evidence are ignored by policy-
> makers (perhaps because it is easier to quibble about methodology than
> it is to address the problem exposed). Given the complexity of
> poverty, each approach can only tell part of the story. But it is striking
> that, whichever you select, it is part of the same story, leading to the
> same conclusion.[24]

• POPULAR DEFINITIONS

Although enormous attention has been paid to the definition of
poverty in expert discussions, so far this does not seem to have
impinged on wider public or political thinking to any significant
extent.

A) PUBLIC DEFINITION OF POVERTY

Attitude surveys suggest that most people still support an absolute
rather than a relative definition of poverty. In 1990 the British Social
Attitudes Survey found that 60 per cent of people agreed that poverty
was about subsistence; 95 per cent, that poverty was about living
below minimum subsistence; and only 25 per cent thought that
poverty was relative to the living standards of others.[25] According to
Peter Golding:

> The most prevalent definition remains the most austere, insisting on
> inadequacy of food and basic living needs before the term becomes
> relevant. The British do like their poor to look the part.[26]

This highlights the commonsense appeal of absolute definitions. As Carey Oppenheim and Lisa Harker say: 'The appeal of an absolute definition of poverty is its apparent clarity and its moral force. Put simply someone is poor if he or she does not have enough to eat'.[27] It also reminds us of the power of political and media definitions, for as Pete Alcock says, 'The public images of poverty are central in determining private perceptions'.[28]

B) POLITICAL DEFINITION

While most social scientists now acknowledge the overlaps between absolute and relative definitions of poverty. this distinction is still central to political and media debates about poverty. It is almost as if it has become a visible way of maintaining the broader political and ideological divisions between left and right. The political right and Conservative governments have generally stood strongly behind subsistence definitions, while the Labour Party and political left have supported relative models. Each new poverty study and report becomes the opportunity for a rerun of this polarised debate. This happened, for example, when the high-profile report of the Joseph Rowntree Income and Wealth Inquiry was published.[29] Labour politicians referred to poverty as a relative concept:

> Of course poverty is relative to the wealth, income and lifestyles of those who live around us. Any other definition of poverty makes no sense at all.[30]

Conversely, Conservative members and government ministers defended a subsistence model, using the argument that increased living standards necessarily lead to a reduction in poverty:

> I sometimes wonder whether the great problem which we face nowadays is not relative poverty but relative prosperity. Why will not many people simply accept that they are getting richer and not count themselves as poor? Why do they seem to get more miserable as they receive more of the supposed material benefits of life ?[31]

Right wing politicians and Conservative administrations have dismissed relative poverty as reflecting no more than inequalities in society. They have used the absolute concept of poverty to suggest that poverty no longer exists in the UK, arguing that the social security system has removed its threat. So in 1989, John Moore, then Secretary of State for Social Services, in a speech titled 'The end of the line for poverty', argued that economic success had put an end to poverty in the UK.[32] This issue was revisited in 1996 when Peter Lilley, as Social Security Secretary, refusing to take measures to counter poverty in response to the UN world summit on social development, wrote that he regarded it as a matter for 'underdeveloped countries' and that Britain already had the mechanisms 'to prevent poverty'[33]

C) MEDIA DEFINITION

There is the same polarised definition of poverty in the media. While left of centre broadsheets like the Guardian, Observer and Independent lend their support to findings based on a relative definition, the right wing press, broadsheets as well as tabloids, are dismissive of it. When, for example, in 1996, the Joseph Rowntree Foundation produced its definitive report drawing together the findings of more than 30 research studies on life on a low income, the Daily Mail's response was:

> Think of a number. Double it. According to the latest report from the Joseph Rowntree Foundation, some 14 million of us are 'people living on low incomes'. In plain English, the report suggests that a quarter of the population is poor. What palpable nonsense.
>
> The only reason that the foundation can get away with plucking such figures out of the air is because it uses a relative measure of deprivation.[34]

LANGUAGE AND IMAGES

Language and images are central in the social construction of any social problem. They are especially important in the case of poverty because it has always been perceived as much in moral terms as in economic, social or political ones. The morality of poor people comes under particular challenge. Over many centuries, policy has categorised them as the 'deserving' and the 'undeserving'. The language and images of poverty have generally reflected rather than transcended this moral divide. They influence people's understanding of poverty and how poor people are presented. As we shall see, they are more often pejorative and demeaning than positive and empowering. Here we focus on four key areas of poverty language and images; the term 'poverty' itself, the idea of the 'underclass' and media and poverty lobby images.

DEBATES AROUND USE OF THE WORD POVERTY

Conservative administrations under Margaret Thatcher and John Major not only questioned the existence of poverty, they also tried to do away with the word itself. Mrs Thatcher forbad ministers to use the 'p' word. 'The word 'poor' was once described by a senior Civil Servant as 'one that the Government actually disputes'.[35] There has been increasing official use of euphemisms and other terms instead since the late 1980s, including, 'low income', 'below average income', 'the bottom ten percent'.

Hartley Dean raises a very different issue about the use of the word; its effect on the people it is used to describe:

> The data from our interviews with social security claimants reveals in its sheer complexity a certain crushing force behind the currency of the 'p' word ... So long as the social distribution of resources remains unequal, 'poverty' as a phantom of discourse is capable of quietly terrorising the entire population.[36]

The ambivalence many in poverty themselves feel about the word (explored further in Chapter 3) was exploited by government ministers in the late 1980s who argued that to use the word is to demean those living on income support. Dean, like Carey Oppenheim and Lisa Harker, concludes that we do still have to use the 'p' word because as they say:

> While it is true that some people living in poverty do not wish to be identified as 'poor', if the word 'poverty' is obliterated from public discussion, the experience of people in poverty disappears from our perception of social reality.[37]

• THE LANGUAGE OF THE 'UNDERCLASS'

Since the 1980s, the idea of the 'underclass' has played a crucial part in the social construction of poverty; its political and media representation and in the legitimation of increasingly harsh policy provisions against poor people.[38] The idea has been used as a catch-all to lump together crime, violence, drug abuse, dependency, lone mothers, black and minority ethnic groups. It is associated with extreme language which plays on people's fears and insecurity, with talk of of cancer, plague, pestilence, illegitimacy and disorder. The fact that its definition has always been vague and defective and that the evidence consistently contradicts the existence of an 'underclass' of poor people who reject the values and aspirations of society at large has not undermined its influence.[39] Significantly, its proponents cut across conventional political divides. While their aims may be different, the effects appear the same; to pathologise, stereotype, demean and stigmatise poor people and 'to write them off as beyond the bonds of common citizenship'.[40] Together with the notion of a 'dependency culture', also not supported by the research evidence, it is now being used as much by a new Labour administration as it was by its Conservative predecessors.

• MEDIA IMAGES

The media's role in maligning poor people is well known. The stereotyping and stigmatisation of claimants by the media, for example, has been thoroughly documented.[41] Tabloids like The Sun and the Daily Mail continue to attack and condemn people in poverty, for instance:

> We are turning into a nation of cheats and spivs. And many of our children are now being brought up to know no other way. The feckless, the workshy, the scroungers, the loafers are laughing all the way to the next Giro cheque.[42]

> The lamentable fact is that many people in this country haven't the faintest idea how to go about improving their own lives or those of their children. They are waiting for Godot ...[43]

> Hundreds of furious readers phoned up our shop-a-cheat hotline after we exposed the scandal of bogus invalids sponging state handouts. Dr Alan Patterson, 43, who tested welfare applicants for the Benefits Agency, claimed in yesterday's Sun that eight out of ten 'invalids' were able to work and were conning £6.2 billion a year on handouts.[44]

Less attention has been paid to media attempts to take a *positive* line on poverty, although there seem to be just as many problems. The media largely only seem able to portray poor people as 'bad' or 'sad'. When TV documentaries, or left-of-centre broadsheets want to challenge stereotypes of the 'undeserving poor', while they sometimes offer images of 'heroic survivors', which few of us are likely to live up to, they more often serve up people in poverty as pathetic, hopeless and crushed, passively accepting their plight rather than doing anything about it. For example: 'It's just depressing sitting here looking at four walls. I sit here watching television. That's all the entertainment I get.'[45] People with experience of poverty are generally confined to talking about their troubles, while non-poor 'experts' are wheeled on to provide analysis and prescriptions.[46] This reflects the conventional 'expert' approach to poverty debate. Whatever the intention, the effect is often counterproductive, reinforcing right wing criticisms that 'the poor' are dependent and incapable of doing anything to improve their own situation.

As part of UN International Year for the Eradication of Poverty, Channel 4 Television ran a *Broke* season, which was heralded as a major media event to 'challenge stereotypes and stimulate debate' about poverty. Sadly it fell into all the usual media traps. Afterwards, Channel 4's controller of factual programmes said that she did 'accept that where there was analysis it (had come) from people who were not poor', but wondered if poor people would be able to ask their own questions and present their own proposals because they would be 'too busy fighting their own day-to-day battles'.[47] The evidence from overlapping groups, for example, disabled and older people, shows that many people are both keen and able to take on such tasks.

The media have rarely looked seriously at their own role in the presentation of poverty. An important exception was *Hard Times*, an episode of The Media Show.[48] Its findings were serious cause for concern. They revealed a shocking picture of media manipulation, stereotyping, trivialisation, inaccuracy and distortion, all combining to reinforce images of people in poverty as helpless, hopeless and different to the rest of 'us'.

• POVERTY LOBBY IMAGES

As Hartley Dean says, when the voices of poor people are heard:

> ... it is usually through the good offices of anti-poverty campaigners who have their own particular impressions of who 'the poor' might be. The discourse of poverty incorporates competing images – of victims and villains, and constructs 'the poor' accordingly.[49]

The fact that campaigns need to raise issues and charities need to raise money, means that the poverty lobby is also locked into other agents involved in poverty debate, particularly, as we have said, the media, This creates strong pressures on the lobby to conform to their grammar of poverty. To resist, demands clear principles and skilful strategies. Chris Pond, at the time director of the Low Pay Unit, talked of being phoned by one paper to get a member of the 'underclass' to interview They said:

> What we'd like ideally is a single parent, preferably one who's got several children all by different fathers.[50]

There is a tradition of poverty lobby images in reports, advertising and campaigns; of showing poor people as victims, represented by coarse-grained black and white photographs. While this highlights the problems, the more positive and assertive images which are now emerging show that there is an alternative. Some of the most dehumanising and exploitative imagery is associated with poverty in Africa and the South. This has encouraged discussion about imagery among anti-poverty organisations which in turn has emphasised the importance of dialogue, of getting close to people and understanding their struggles, and of making the political connections and then linking this with different approaches to fundraising and campaigning.[51]

CAUSES AND SOLUTIONS OF POVERTY

If there is little agreement about the definition of poverty, there is even less about its causes and solutions. There are very different ways of approaching the discussion. Carey Oppenheim and Lisa Harker, for example, offer a straightforward analysis of the causes of poverty:

> Poverty in the UK is largely determined by three factors – access to the labour market, extra costs, and the failure of policies to deal with them…Poverty is caused by not having access to decently paid employment. It is also the result of the extra costs of having a child or a disability. Poverty is particularly acute when these two factors combine. Moreover the social security system often fails to meet adequately the needs generated by unemployment, low pay, having a child or (being disabled). Thus poverty is also caused by policies – ie, it is avoidable, not just the consequence of random misfortune. The risk of poverty is not shared out evenly – it depends on social class, on gender and on race.[52]

This last point reflects the increasing recognition in recent years of the relationship between poverty and social divisions of gender, 'race', age and disability.[53] The key common features associated with such poverty are the discrimination which each group faces and the failure of policy either to address this discrimination or meet the groups' particular needs.[54]

The causes and solutions of poverty tend to be interpreted and presented in *ideological* terms. The assumptions and values reflected in competing left and right ideologies are of central importance in shaping both our understanding of poverty and the policy responses that have been made to it. While right wing ideology has been essentially individualistic, focussing on the part the individual plays in his or her poverty; the focus of left wing ideology has been structural, looking at the role of society and broader social, economic, political and cultural relations.

The 'dependency culture' and 'behavioural poverty' theory of the new right has become a dominant strand in the interpretation of poverty in the UK. It both blames poor people for contributing to their own downfall through their own behaviour and attitudes and condemns the welfare state for encouraging 'dependency', hindering wealth creation and increasing public expenditure. While state intervention and redistribution have been the traditional solutions to poverty advanced by the old Labour Party and the left, the new right argues for reduced welfare expenditure and a shift to the private market, to make possible a bigger economy whose benefits will then 'trickle down' to raise the living standards of poor people. New Labour also talks the language of the 'dependency culture' rather than its old language of redistribution. These shifts in political perceptions of causes and solutions have fundamental implications for the politics of poverty.

THE POLITICS OF POVERTY

Poverty has always been a political concept. As Pete Alcock says:

> Many people, including academics, campaigners and politicians, talk about the problem of poverty; and underlying their discussion is the assumption that identifying the problem provides a basis for action on which all will agree. However ... people do not all agree on what the problem of poverty is, and thus, not surprisingly, the action they wish to encourage or justify is not at all the same thing. Most people of course claim that their understanding of poverty is the correct one, based on logical argument or scientific research. But ... there is no one correct, scientific agreed definition because poverty is inevitably a political concept and thus inherently a contested one.[55]

The political nature of poverty and of all the main aspects of poverty debate which we have discussed, has become increasingly explicit in recent years. This has intensified as the dominant politics have moved to the right. Conservative governments developed increasingly narrow definitions of poverty and restrictive benefits policies, including incapacity benefit, jobseekers allowance and ending benefit for asylum seekers.[56] The far right's proposals for poverty have grown more and more severe – echoing recent policy developments in the US, with talk of ending claimants' benefit entitlement after a fixed period and even enforced adoption for lone parent claimants refusing them benefit for a further child.

What change there has been in conventional political positions, has mainly been in realignments on the left, which some critics have interpreted as a shift to the right. The Labour Party has adopted an increasingly pragmatic approach to poverty, based more on highlighting the damaging social and economic effects on the wider society of poor people outside the labour market, than on traditional moral concerns about their predicament.[57] It has explicitly disassociated itself from its longstanding commitment to redistribution through the tax-benefits system. This has been justified in the name of tackling the roots of poverty through a 'welfare to work strategy'. In its appeal to 'middle England', New Labour is distancing itself from its earlier image as the party of 'the poor'. What is not yet clear is whether 'stakeholding' under the New Labour government will mean social cohesion achieved through social control and enforced recruitment to low paid employment, or everyone having a genuine stake in the economy and participating fully in society. Similarly we have still to see whether New Labour's 'community' will fully and equally include poor people, or merely hold them responsible for its problems and breakdown.[58]

As poverty discussion has become more explicitly political, there are growing signs that traditional approaches to anti-poverty debate and action are no longer working. For example, Rowntree's 1995 *Income and Wealth* inquiry, with a broadbased membership, was a self-conscious attempt to get beyond party politics, but it still fell foul of right wing press and politicians and was dismissed by some on the right as partisan, inaccurate and invalid.[59] Two high profile reports in 1996 providing definitive pictures of poverty in the UK, received the same dismissive response in some quarters.[60] Major research highlighting the inadequacy of 'dependency culture' theory and, the idea of the 'underclass' has had minimal impact on political debates about either of them.[61]

What seems to be emerging is a sharpening of the distinctions between the different images presented of poor people: as 'bad' or at least lazy, irresponsible, or incapable and to be blamed on the one hand; or as sad and to be pitied on the other. But underpinning both sides of this divide is the poor cast as 'other', as the objects, not the subjects of the politics of poverty. As we explain in the next chapter, Poverty First Hand is an attempt to redress the balance.

NOTES

1   T Novak, *Rethinking Poverty,* Critical Social Policy, 44/45. 1995, pp58-74.
2   see, for instance, B Jordan, A Theory of Poverty and Exclusion, Polity Press, 1996; F Williams with J Pillinger, *New Thinking on Social Policy Research into Inequality, Social Exclusion and Poverty,* in J Millar and J Bradshaw, (editors), Social Welfare Systems: Towards a Research Agenda, University of Bath/ESRC, 1996
3   P Alcock, *Understanding Poverty,* Macmillian, 1993, p209.
4   S MacGregor, *The Politics of Poverty,* Longman, 1981, p147.
5   P F Whiteley and S J Winyard, *Pressure for the Poor,* Methuen, 1987, p27.
6   See note 5, p56.
7   P Hildrew, *No News is Bad News: Poverty according to the Fleet Street agenda is not 'newsworthy'. Why not?,* New Statesman & Society, 10 June 1988, pp27-28.
8   cited in P Golding and S Middleton, *Images of Welfare: Press and public attitudes to poverty,* Blackwell and Robertson, 1982, p143.
9   Daily Mail, *Don't Bash the Benefit Claiments, Says Report,* 4 June 1997.
10 For example, A Lazzeri and B Proctor, *Lazy Single Mum is a Disgrace. She Should Quit Cigs ... and Find Work,* The Sun, 6 June 1997.
11 P Beaumont, *Give Britain a New Deal: Suspicion greets Gordon's tough love,* Observer, 6 July 1997.
12 See note 3, p57.
13 For a useful overview, see, J Roll, *Understanding Poverty,* Family Policy Studies Centre, 1992.
14 See note 4, p62.
15 C Walker and A Walker, Poverty and the Poor, in M Haralambos (editor), Developments in Sociology, Causeway Press, 1994, pp43-48.
16 See note 3, p58.
17 P Townsend, *Poverty in the United Kingdom,* Penguin, 1979, p31.
18 See note 15, p45.
19 See note 3, pp57-74.
20 See note 15, p48.
21 See note 3, p62
22 R Walker and S Middleton, *Defining Poverty Lines: Reaching consensus through negotiation,* Benefits, No 14, September-October 1995, pp20-21.
23 See note 3, p73.

24 C Oppenheim and L Harker, *Poverty: the Facts,* Revised and updated third edition, CPAG, 1996, pvi.

25 P Taylor-Gooby, *Social Welfare: The unkindest cuts,* in R Jowell and others (editors), British Social Attitudes, the Seventh Report, 1990.

26 P Golding, *Poor Attitudes,* in S Becker (editor), Windows of Opportunity, CPAG, 1991, pp39-54.

27 See note 24, p8.

28 See note 3, p19.

29 P Beresford and D A Green, *Income and Wealth: An opportunity to reassess the UK poverty debate?,* Crtical Social Policy, Issue 46, Spring 1996, pp95-109.

30 Hansard, 6-10 February 1995, col.873.

31 As above col.872.

32 J Moore, The End of the Line for Poverty, speech to the Greater London Area Conservative Party Conference, 11 May 1989.

33 D Brindle, *Charities' UN Protest over British Poverty: Ministers 'fail to honour social pledges',* Guardian, 22 May 1996.

34 Daily Mail, *Comment: Poverty Trap,* June 4 1996.

35 See note 24, p12.

36 H Dean, *Poverty Discourse and the Disempowerment of the Poor,* Critical Social Policy, Issue 35, Autumn 1992, pp79-88.

37 See note 24, p13.

38 K Mann, *Watching the Defectives: Observers of the underclass in the USA, Britain and Australia,* Critical Social Policy, Issue 41, Autumn 1994, pp79-99.

39 E Kempson, *Life on a Low Income,* Joseph Rowntree Foundation, 1996.

40 R Lister, *The Exclusive Society: Citizenship and the poor,* CPAG, 1990. See also R Lister, *In Search of the 'Underclass',* Introduction to Charles Murray and the Underclass Debate, IEA Health and Welfare Unit, 1996.

41 See note 8.

42 The Sun, 10 June 1995.

43 A Daniels, *Commentary: Handouts that will never be passport to riches: drawbacks of dependency,* Daily Mail, 4 June 1996.

44 C Staples and A Walton, *The Scam Busters: Hundreds of readers phone up our hotline to shop dole fiddlers.* The Sun, 11 June 1997.

45 Independent, *Comment,* 10 February 1995.

46 P Beresford and S Croft, *Its Our Problem Too!: Challenging the exclusion of poor people from poverty discourse,* Critical Social Policy, Issue 44/45, Autumn 1995, pp75-95.

47 Personal Communication, 11 July 1996.

48 The Media Show, Hard Times, Channel 4 Television, 17 March 1991.

49 See note 36, p81.

50 R Lister and P Beresford, *Working Together Against Poverty: Involving poor people in action against poverty,* Open Services Project and Department of Applied Social Studies, University of Bradford, 1991, p17.

51 S Nyoni, *Images of Poverty: A view from Zimbabwe,* Poverty, The Journal of the Child Poverty Action Group, Issue 71, 1988/89, pp6-12.

52 See note 24, pp47, 63.

53 See note 3.

54 See note 24.

55 See note 3, p3.

56 C Oppenheim and R Lister, *Ten Years After the Social Security Act 1986,* in M May, E Brunsden and G Craig (editors), Social Policy Review 8, Social Policy Association, 1996.

57 See note 29, pp104-105.

58 R Lister, *Whose Community?,* Community Care, 29 May – 4 June 1997, p25.

59 See note 29.

60 See notes 24 and 39.

61 For example H Dean and P Taylor-Gooby, *Dependency Culture: The explosion of a myth,* Harvester Wheatsheaf, 1992; and E Kempson, *Life on a Low Income,* Joseph Rowntree Foundation, 1996.

2

Poverty at First Hand
The involvement of people with experience of poverty

POOR PEOPLE'S EXCLUSION

One key group has been conspicuous by its absence so far in poverty discussion and policy development – people with experience of poverty themselves. The previous chapter demonstrated how the four key agents involved in poverty debate – academics, the poverty lobby, politicians and media – largely don't include people with experience of poverty. The poverty debate has also been characterised more generally by poor people's exclusion. They have rarely been included in discussions about the key focuses of dominant debates; the definition, language and imagery, causes and solutions of poverty. Little is known, therefore, about what they think about the definition of poverty; who if anyone they would include as poor, their feelings about language and imagery, or their analysis of and policy proposals for poverty. Instead, people with experience of poverty have mainly been confined to talking about being poor. When their views have been included, it has usually been to evidence and flesh out other people's viewpoints, arguments and analysis.

The exclusion of people with experience of poverty from poverty debates and developments is perhaps surprising for three reasons. First, because on all current measures, they are a very large minority, numbering many millions, of which some would certainly be expected to have something to say.[1] Second, since there is little agreement about poverty and people's view of it largely seems to be shaped by their own ideological and material relation to poverty, one might expect those people in the closest relationship with it to have a central and interesting perspective to bring to the discussion. Third, other oppressed groups are increasingly shaping public and political debates about their position in society and their rights and needs. Groups like mental health service users and disabled people have long faced comparable, if not greater stigma to people included as poor and yet they have increasingly become part of discussions to change their situation.

THE IMPORTANCE OF AN INCLUSIVE POVERTY DEBATE

For a long time, the exclusion of people with experience of poverty from poverty debates and development passed without comment. In 1989, Paul Wilding noted '(the) voices of the poor are seldom heard'.[2] In recent years, however, particularly in the past decade, the issue has begun to emerge more clearly.[3] Discussion and experience are beginning to show why it matters if poor people aren't included in poverty discourse and what the gains might be if they were.

Before looking at these in more detail, there is one further point we would like, as authors, to make clear. We believe that people with experience of poverty have a particular contribution to make to poverty discussions and anti-poverty action and that they should have an equal chance to make it. They don't have the only insight into poverty, but they have particular knowledge and understanding of and concern about their oppression, just as women, black people, lesbians and gay men, disabled people and others do of theirs. So far, poor people have had few chances to contribute to discussions about poverty or to come together to develop their own.

At the same time, we are not saying that *only* poor people have something to say about poverty, or that they alone have a right to talk or write about it. It is not our view that only the views of people with experience of poverty are valid or should be listened to, or that the discussion of poverty should be confined to them. Instead we want to stress the importance of an *inclusive* approach to poverty, which recognises the validity of *all* voices seeking to challenge poverty. We are not suggesting that old exclusions should be replaced with new ones. We are making the case for debates and developments about poverty which include people with experience of poverty and don't specifically exclude them. Their particular insights, experience, knowledge and understanding are important and should not be lost. It is also important to remember that there is unlikely to be one view among people with experience of poverty. The similarities and differences that exist among people who are poor should be recognised, as well as those between them and other groups involved in poverty debates. Our overall concern here is to help develop an open and inclusive debate about poverty which makes it possible for the insights, experience and ideas of all groups committed to the eradication of poverty to be drawn in, shared and provide a basis for action.

There are strong arguments for including people with experience of poverty in poverty debates and policy development. Three central ones are emerging.

• BETTER INFORMED POVERTY DEBATE

The involvement of recipients of public policy in other fields has repeatedly been shown to improve its ability to promote their rights and meet their needs.[4] Their first hand knowledge and experience offers an invaluable basis for developing needs-led policy and practice. The same is true for anti-poverty action and discussion. The poverty debate will be better informed if those affected are part of it. Their involvement makes it possible for the debate to identify, reflect and advance their needs, concerns and interests more accurately and closely. Poor people's involvement makes possible more relevant and participatory research and analysis. It is likely to lead to more effective methods and appropriate subjects for campaigning. In a context of limited public and anti-poverty resources, it can contribute to a more rational and democratic basis for priority setting.

• STRONGER AND MORE EFFECTIVE ANTI-POVERTY ACTION

Anti-poverty discussions and campaigns without the involvement of poor people are having only limited success. The lesson of recent politics is that *popular* discussions and campaigns are the ones which seem to make the most impact. Expressions of this new participatory politics can be seen in campaigns for disabled people's rights, the environment and against road building as well as in the black people's, gay men and lesbians' movements. Whereas poverty campaigns and the poverty lobby do not necessarily even have the support of their chosen constituency, such campaigns mobilise large numbers of people, gain popular support and are not narrowly associated with a particular political or party interest. Such broad-based campaigns and their successes stand in contrast with narrowly based anti-poverty campaigns and their difficulties under Conservative administrations in the 1980s and 1990s. Where there have been more broad-based campaigns associated with poverty, for example against the poll tax[5] and the Child Support Act, these have been much more successful, although the latter's success in winning a number of concessions in favour of absent fathers, is overlaid with issues around the power of middle class male agendas and interests.[6] The long-term political impact of broad-based anti-poverty campaigns involving poor people themselves could be considerable.

• RESPECTING THE RIGHTS AND CITIZENSHIP OF POOR PEOPLE

Including poor people in poverty discussions challenges the exclusion which anti-poverty campaigners rightly condemn as a central effect of impoverishment. Their inclusion is part of the broader issue of addressing the restricted citizenship of people who are poor. It also signifies respect for poor people; an acknowledgement that they have something to offer, that their contribution is important, worthwhile and valued, and recognition of their expertise in their own experience. Much of the social democratic/social administration debate about poverty has focused on equality. Supporting people to speak for themselves is a basic requirement for such equality. It is an extension of the moral argument long offered by the poverty lobby that something should be done about poverty. It makes it possible for poor people themselves to be involved in doing something about it and in challenging their social exclusion. It also offers a practical corrective to myths about a 'dependency culture', making it possible for people to challenge stereotypes of themselves as passive, lazy and incapable. Poor people thus cease to be 'the other' lacking 'expert status on their own lives' and become instead commentators and analysts.[7]

This is an important time to include people with experience of poverty in poverty discourse. It is a time of fundamental social, economic and political change, fed by 'globalisation', political realignments, electoral change and new technology. These are having a fundamental impact on the lives of everyone, exposing people who were previously unaffected to new uncertainties and new risks of poverty. The future of welfare and the welfare state are both uncertain. New ideas, like 'social exclusion' have been introduced into the debate, carrying with them their own problems and possibilities.[8] It is crucial that such debates and developments now engage with and are informed by poor people themselves.

LEARNING FROM THE DISABLED PEOPLE'S MOVEMENT

If the arguments for involving people with experience of poverty in poverty debates and anti-poverty action are strong, doubts are still frequently expressed about the practicality of doing so. Concerns have been raised about whether people with experience of poverty would want to be involved, and have the energy to do so – given the massive pressures they are under – or the skills that are needed. The disabled people's movement offers a powerful example to counter such arguments. Disabled people are especially exposed to poverty, but their movement shows that involving people with experience of poverty is feasible and that their involvement is likely to make a strong and helpful impact on anti-poverty discussions and developments. The disabled people's movement has organised around peoples' *disablement* by society, rather than by campaigning on the isolated issue of poverty.

The disabled people's movement has transformed disability debates and policy. It has redefined disability, with the development of its 'social model' of disability;[9] developed its own language of disability; challenged dominant media images;[10] established its own arts and culture; and generated its own sophisticated analysis and strategies.[11] The disabled people's movement has set up its own broad-based democratically constituted local, national and international organisations, under the control of disabled people. It has, with some success, campaigned in the UK for anti-discrimination legislation and direct payments legislation giving disabled people control over the personal assistance they receive. The disabled people's movement has both changed the terms of debate about disability, transforming it from a welfare to a rights issue, and become an effective political force. It has achieved this through both parliamentary and extra-parliamentary action, including direct action, both in the UK and internationally.

INVOLVING PEOPLE WITH EXPERIENCE OF POVERTY

Although poor people remain excluded from much anti-poverty action and debate, there is a long, largely hidden, history of poor people struggling to be part of discussions about poverty and being poor and of policy developments affecting them.[12] More recently, in the UK in the 1960s and 1970s, there was a highly visible and vocal movement of claimant unions.[13] There were comparable developments in the US around the same time extending to legislation to include representatives of poor people on local governing boards of 'programs for the poor'.[14]

More recently, disabled activists have been among the first to argue for the involvement of poor people in anti-poverty debates.[15] Much of the involvement of people with experience of poverty has been around practical initiatives for self-help and mutual aid. There are now also a growing number of initiatives where poor people are beginning to be involved in poverty discussions, particularly at local level. It will be helpful to look more closely at some key examples.

THE GREATER LONDON CLAIMANTS COMMISSION

The Claimants Commission was set up in 1985 by the Greater London Council. Its aim was to find out about claimants' experience of the social security system in London and how they thought it was working. All 12 members of the Commission were themselves claimants, almost all without any previous experience of such involvement. They were a very mixed group in terms of age, 'race', gender, disability and kind of benefit they received. The Commission was well resourced, with its own office and secretariat. Members were valued for their experience and equal participation was ensured by providing full expenses to cover travel, child care and other needs. Members of the Commission sought training and carried out their own consultations and research and produced their own report.[16]

WOMEN AND POVERTY IN THE EUROPEAN COMMUNITY

This initiative was organised by the European Network of Women. In 1988 more than 150 women with experience of poverty from the member states, including the United Kingdom, came together in Brussels to give testimony and develop demands for policy change in the EC. In 1991 there was a follow-up meeting in Copenhagen, in which women with experience of poverty came together in a smaller group, from just some of the EC countries. As well as highlighting the similarity and diversity of issues facing different women and operating in different countries; the meetings demonstrated the value of being able to share experience internationally, and the importance of ensuring the inclusion of women of diverse backgrounds, irrespective of age, 'race', disability and sexuality.[17]

WORKING TOGETHER AGAINST POVERTY

This national one day meeting in York in 1990 brought together people with experience of poverty and anti-poverty professionals to discuss the involvement of poor people in anti-poverty action. The aim was for people to be able to hear each other's points of view and see if there were things they might be able to do together. The meeting showed there was considerable common ground and that the two groups could talk to and learn from each other. Participants talked about the obstacles to involvement and involving people for the future. Everyone seemed to find the day useful and enjoyable and there was general agreement that it was a discussion which needed to be continued.[18]

ATD FOURTH WORLD

ATD Fourth World has been working for nearly 40 years in Europe and other continents 'to enable the poor to come together and contribute to the development of a society that includes the poorest in its plans and progress'. It describes its approach as to work *with* the very poor, rather than *for* them. Partnership is a key concept in the work of ATD Fourth World, which includes local community, educational and cultural programmes with poor people. It sees the poorest people as 'creative partners in the process of change', with poor people themselves acting as 'expert witnesses'. ATD Fourth World places an emphasis on poor people developing skills and confidence and speaking for themselves.[19]

CHURCH ACTION ON POVERTY

Church Action on Poverty was set up in 1982 as a national ecumenical response to poverty in Britain. In 1994, it established the *Local People National Voice* project. The aims of this project were to provide opportunities for people with direct experience of poverty 'to speak out for themselves, to raise awareness locally and nationally and create an effective dialogue between policy makers, church members and people experiencing poverty and to inform Church Action on Poverty's own work.'[20]

Local People National Voice consisted of a series of events and hearings at which people with experience of poverty could speak out about their experiences and ideas, culminating in a national poverty hearing in March 1996 which received considerable media coverage. The Hearing was in two parts; in the morning speakers talked about their own experience of poverty and how they coped and in the afternoon they talked about some of the initiatives they were taking 'to improve their situation'.[21] As part of the *Local People National Voice* project, Church Action on Poverty set up a small policy group, made up mainly of people with experience of poverty and produced a short report giving the group's own initial analysis of poverty and ideas for improving policy.[22]

CITIZENS' COMMISSION ON THE FUTURE OF THE WELFARE STATE

The Citizens's Commission was set up to provide an opportunity for welfare state service users to work out what kind of welfare state they wanted for the future. The Commission, which was independent, was made up of people who were themselves users of welfare state services, including lone parents, disabled and older people, people with learning difficulties, people living on benefits and low income, carers and other groups over-represented in poverty. The Commission's part-time worker was also a welfare state service user. Members of the Commission met with and received evidence from groups of welfare state service users nationwide. They undertook their own research and analysis and produced their own book-length report. For the first time people with direct experience of poverty were able to set their *own* views and proposals for the future of welfare next to 'expert' and political reports.[23]

UK COALITION AGAINST POVERTY

This initiative was originally established to advance the aims of the UN International Year for the Eradication of Poverty in the UK. The Coalition's coordinating committee included members of large charities and voluntary organisations as well as of smaller community and user-led organisations and people with experience of poverty.

The involvement of people with experience of poverty was both a central principle and objective of the Coalition. It made a commitment to support their involvement in all its activities and decisions. It organised a national participation event to enable people with experience of poverty to exchange their knowledge, experience and ideas.[24] It also initiated the setting up of an All Party Parliamentary Committee on Poverty and established an information project to produce campaign materials in association with people with experience of poverty.[25] It was reconstituted as the UK Coalition Against Poverty in the wake of the declaration of a UN Decade for the Eradication of Poverty at the end of 1996, with an elected coordinating group with the aim of having 50% representation of people with direct experience of poverty.

EMERGING ISSUES

Between them, these initiatives to involve poor people in the development of poverty discussion and action, add up to a considerable body of experience. They make it possible to draw some initial conclusions about involving poor people. These include the following:

- Involving people with experience of poverty can be done. It is a practical and feasible policy, which is valued both by poor people and anti-poverty professionals and can offer gains to both.
- There is now clear evidence that many poor people are willing and able to become involved in poverty debates and developments, given the opportunity and support.
- There is no one way of involving people with experience of poverty, but rather a range of different approaches offering different degrees and kinds of involvement. Some existing initiatives are concerned with enabling people to give testimony, others to undertake their own research, develop their own discussion and formulate their own demands.
- The involvement of poor people, like all participatory initiatives, is not necessarily easy. It can be particularly difficult given the heterogeneous nature of the poor population and the stigma associated with the label 'poverty'. Anti-poverty professionals and people with experience of poverty often have different expectations, ideas and assumptions about participation and these

can create misunderstanding, conflict and difficulties. But there is also the possibility for learning and exchange between them which can make it possible to overcome these obstacles and make progress together.

- Involving people with experience of poverty requires new skills and changed social relations between poor people and anti-poverty organisations. There is growing experience to provide the basis for both.

- While it is often easier to start at local level – where people are – the voices of poor people can have a powerful impact at national level.

The initiatives we have described are indicative of a broader shift and interest which is emerging in the politics of poverty. Voluntary organisations which are involved in anti-poverty work, like Family Service Units, Barnardo's and Save the Children are taking an increasingly active interest in 'user involvement' in their work.[26] Funders and academic researchers are addressing this in related fields like community care. Local authorities are beginning to recognise the need for poor peoples' participation in anti-poverty strategies.[27] Anti-poverty organisations are beginning to press for the broader involvement of people with experience of poverty. In its Scottish Declaration On Poverty, for example, the Scottish Anti-Poverty Network calls on government, social and economic agencies to 'involve people living in poverty in all decisions which affect them.'[28] Partnership with those affected by poverty is also a theme at European level in the pronouncements both of the European Commission and the European Anti-Poverty Network.

These developments suggest that the involvement of people with experience of poverty is now at last on the poverty agenda. There is no agreement about it. It still has many critics and faces many objections. There are many problems still to be addressed. But poor people are beginning to have a presence in poverty debates and to make their voices heard, and not just as illustrations for someone else's points.

POVERTY FIRST HAND

The Poverty First Hand project on which this book is based is part of this new tradition of involving poor people in anti-poverty discussion and action. It grew out of the meeting in York, which two of us organised, bringing together anti-poverty professionals and people with experience of poverty. Participants were keen that the enthusiasm and impetus gained by this meeting should not be lost and that the progress made should be taken further. The five main issues which participants explored at that meeting were:

- the causes of poverty
- the definition of poverty: what it means and the effects of using the term
- the effects of poverty
- how poverty and poor people are presented publicly
- campaigning and involving poor people

These areas were adopted as the focus for the Poverty First Hand project to build on participants' priorities.

It may be helpful at this point, to clarify the similarities and differences between this project and traditional approaches to poverty research, by locating it in its broader research context.

There is a long history of research on poverty and poor people. Much of it has been in the tradition of exploring the extent and effects of poverty. More recently, poor people have been asked their views, but predominantly about their experience of poverty and its effects on them.[29] The research agenda has still been set by outside researchers, however, and poor people have mainly served as a data source. A further development in research provides a bridge linking more traditional approaches with the kind of participatory approach which we have sought to adopt in this project. It has done this by using more qualitative research methods;[30] by enabling poor people themselves to offer their interpretations and views of their personal situation[31] and by drawing on research undertaken by groups with particular experience of poverty, for example, people with learning difficulties.[32]

A NEW APPROACH TO RESEARCH

A growing dissatisfaction with traditional approaches to the analysis of poverty is now also emerging from some poverty academics and there is a search for new theories of poverty.[33] These have, however, largely maintained the traditional social relations of inquiry, with commentators and analysts offering their own ideas and proposals. But there is also beginning to be recognition that such an exclusive approach to analysis may actually be part of the broader problem of poverty, which itself may be better understood in terms of the social relations of power and the unequal distribution of power, rather than of material goods.[34] Members of the disabled people's movement, in the related context of disability research, have also highlighted the destructive effects of traditional research relations.[35]

The key objectives of the Poverty First Hand project were to enable the fuller participation of people with experience of poverty and to make it possible for them to speak for themselves, rather than just inform the analysis and arguments of others. Thus the project was crucially different in *purpose* and *process* to traditional poverty research, while located in the growing tradition of participatory and emancipatory research. Before we look in more detail at the methodology and method of the project, it may be helpful to headline some of the key components that characterised its approach. These include:

- poor people playing a part in shaping the research agenda – the project took forward the issues raised by participants at the York meeting organised by two of the authors;
- poor people going beyond reporting their personal experience;
- enabling poor people to offer their own own analysis, ideas and proposals;
- the use of group discussions rather than individual interviews to help equalise the research relationship and to counter the individualisation of analysis;
- enabling participants to include their own concerns in discussion;
- attempting to involve participants in the editorial process of the research report;
- prioritising the research as a basis for action by and involving people with experience of poverty. This book is seen as one stage in a continuing process of working for change involving poor people.

The fact that we adopted a different approach to poverty research has not meant that our research findings are necessarily different to those of other research. In some cases, the findings are similar, for example, over the effects of poverty, where existing findings and our research reinforce each other, although there are also some new insights. But this project has also covered new ground which has not so far been explored by conventional researchers. It provides new information, for example, about how poor people see poverty and what their proposals are for challenging it. *All* the findings presented here can also be seen as new because they emerge from a different research process. In this project people with experience of poverty have had the chance to identify and develop *their* concerns, priorities and interpretations, instead of just responding to those of outside researchers. When, for example, they speak of the problems that Christmas and holidays pose for people who are poor, or the damaging physical and mental effects of being poor, it is they, rather than researchers, who have raised the issue.

RESEARCH METHODOLOGY AND METHODS

We now present in greater detail the rationale of the project and its research methods (see also Appendix 1 for further information).

As we said in the information which we gave to participants:

> People on low income and groups especially affected by poverty have generally had little chance so far to say what they think about the subject. The aim of this project is to change this by providing a chance for people with first hand experience of the issues associated with poverty to tell their side of the story.

We wanted to enable people with experience of poverty to take part in and contribute their views to existing poverty discussion and hopefully help it to develop, rather than set the agenda for them. The focus of the project was therefore the key elements that have made up this discussion (see Chapter 1). The issues we discussed with people with experience of poverty were:

- the definition of poverty – people's views of dominant definitions as well as their own conceptualisation of poverty;
- their views on the causes of poverty;
- their views on the effects of poverty;
- the images and language of poverty;
- their views of the media and political presentation of poverty;
- their proposals for action on poverty, including the role of people with experience of poverty

The aim of Poverty First Hand has been to help make possible the fuller and more equal participation of people with experience of poverty in poverty debates and anti-poverty action. Because of this, it was important that the research project should be as participatory as possible. We wanted people's participation in the project to be an empowering experience and not reflect the many negative aspects of people's lives when they are poor. We wanted, therefore, to use a research methodology and research methods which were consistent with this, although we had to scale down our aspirations because of funding limitations.

There are two new linked approaches to research – participatory and emancipatory. These closely reflect the aspirations we had and our project was based on them.[36] They place an emphasis on:

- equalising the relationship between research and its subjects;
- linking research with action for change.

As Alan Stanton says:

> Participatory research ... challenges inequality by supporting people in the creation of their own knowledge ... Its rationale is their right to participate actively in processes affecting their lives. Writers on participatory research often see this link between research and action as its characteristic feature.[37]

These were major objectives for us. We wanted the results of the project to be circulated at local and national level, to have an influence on the poverty debate and to be available for anti-poverty agencies and groups and organisations involving and controlled by people with experience of poverty to use to help in their work and campaigning.

We also wanted to use a research method consistent with a participatory research approach. We adopted the method of group discussions. We had considerable experience of this method and we knew that it helped put research participants in a stronger relationship to the research process through giving them the confidence and assertiveness that comes from being with each other and because it helped them to develop their own discussion, bouncing views and ideas off each other.

The discussions were based on a semi-structured schedule, (see Appendix 3) developed on the basis of previous experience of working with people who were poor. It was designed to gain participants' views and ideas about key issues in current poverty debates, using a flexible framework which also provided scope for groups to explore their own particular interests and concerns. The framework was developed by the researchers and built on what people with experience of poverty had said at the York meeting. Thus while groups covered the same general ground, they also developed their own particular discussions, reflecting their particular concerns and interests.

With participants' agreement, the discussions were tape recorded and then transcribed. They were then returned to participants to make any comments or changes they wished and participants later received a copy of the draft text including their comments to check, change and agree.

It should be noted that this project was carried out and group discussions undertaken while the Conservative government was in power. When participants refer to the government and government policy, they are thus referring to Conservative government. This should not, however, be taken to mean that their comments are any less relevant now; traditional differences between Labour and Conservative have become blurred in recent years and many participants were suspicious of all political parties and of government generally.

THE PEOPLE TAKING PART IN THE PROJECT

We carried out a series of 20 group discussions with people who had current or previous experience of poverty. We explained clearly what we were doing to people so that their participation could be on the basis of their informed consent. In undertaking the research, we found we had to deal with a paradox which might make it very difficult for people with experience of poverty ever to offer their ideas and views about poverty. How do you know who to include? How do you avoid pre-empting people's own conceptualisation of poverty in who is included? Our concern was to enable people who would be likely to be included in the administrative category of 'poverty' and 'being poor', to offer their views and ideas.

Since the definition of poverty was one of the issues which we wanted to explore in the project, we did not draw it too tightly. We did not want to impose a narrow definition as a kind of admission test, which might exclude some people who saw themselves as poor and pre-judge the issue. Instead we relied essentially on people's self-definition. Groups took part who associated themselves with the issue of poverty. This is an approach which has been helpfully used by related social movements, like the disabled people's and psychiatric system survivors' movements.[38] Such an approach makes it possible for issues and questions around definition to be developed in the research, rather than anticipated by it. It did, however, also present a problem as some groups or individuals did not want to identify with the label 'poor' in the first place (see also Chapter 3 and Appendix 1). This comment from one woman highlights the complexity of poor people's own definition and conceptualisation of poverty which we report in more detail in the next chapter:

> I'm not poor now, but if you look at this poverty line, I'm still below the poverty line, but I no longer see myself as poor. That's because I have been really, really poor and I'm no longer poor...I'm disabled now, so I've been given Disability Living Allowance...I can't go out because then you've got to have a baby-sitter as well as beer money...(But) I don't have to say wait until next week. I don't have to miss a meal for new school clothes anymore. I am quite prepared to say I have been poor. I'm still poor according to everybody else, but I can manage now. (Women's education group)

We can be confident that almost all, if not all participants had first hand experience of poverty, as conventionally defined in policy and practice and that in most cases it was current experience.

We wanted to include as wide a range of poor people as possible to represent the variety of experience and perspectives which they reflect. We were also anxious to ensure that women, Black people and minority ethnic groups were fully represented, although we were only partially successful on the latter count. Participants came from many parts of the country; they included people on benefits, lone parents, young and older people, homeless people, people with small children, unemployed people, mental health service users, young offenders and people living in town and country. There were large and small groups. There were also some groups we did not manage to involve, for example, travellers and people on low wages.

We tried to identify and include groups in the project in as systematic and representative a way as possible, to reflect the diversity of people included as poor. Most were existing groups, rather than groups brought together for the purpose of this project, so they had their own identity and history. Groups were identified by a range of criteria which were relevant both in reflecting the diversity of people who experience poverty and the different reasons for which people who are poor may come together. Thus we included groups which existed on the basis of age, including both young and old people; groups which came together because of the concerns and nature of family, including lone parent groups and family groups; groups related to the provision of support, including both self-help and mutual aid groups and groups associated with services providing support; women's groups which were concerned with poverty issues and whose members were poor; claimant based groups, including groups of unemployed people; interest or identity groups, for example groups of homeless and disabled people and people who use mental health services, and local or community-based groups, for example, residents and tenants groups.

People who took part in the project came to it in a variety of ways; through involvement in self-help, support, self-advocacy and campaigning groups and through use of services and amenities for poor people and disadvantaged areas. There were also, of course, overlaps between groups. Some campaigning groups were concerned with anti-poverty action; others were organised around other issues. Thus the project included, for example, members of a LETS (local exchange trading system) group, where people offer each other goods and services without exchange of money; members of a women's adult education project, members of a centre for unemployed people and young people who used an accommodation and advice project for homeless young people. (See Appendix 2 for full details of participating groups)

We do not claim that participants in the project were representative of all poor people, but we did involve a wide range of people with experience of poverty, more diverse indeed than many conventional studies which have focused on claimants and recipients of welfare services. The issue of 'representativeness' is frequently raised when members of groups experiencing oppression express their views, or their views are reported in research like this. Their representativeness is called into question. This is particularly likely to be the case if people take part in campaigning or are actively involved in any way. Although some participants in the project were involved in campaigning, more were not. For example, people were included on the basis of being young offenders, as well as through being involved in campaigning. While such involvement might affect what they said, what evidence there is suggests that contrary to some conventional assumptions, people who are actively involved tend to express similar views to those who are not, although they may be able to act more effectively on them[39] (see Appendix 1).

A QUALITATIVE RESEARCH PROJECT

Because this is a qualitative rather than quantitative study, we have generally not tried to quantify the responses of participants. We have sought to avoid any spurious suggestion of statistical significance. However, where there was a strong response to an issue, or where most groups held a particular view, we have noted this accordingly, to indicate the direction of opinion. There were also agreements and disagreements within groups and sometimes we have been able to give a feel of these by including exchanges that took place. We have included comments which were typical of many more. Sometimes only one person might make a particular point, but there would be agreement from others. An isolated comment therefore certainly did not necessarily mean an isolated view in a group and where we have included such comments, unless we have indicated otherwise, this is the case. Such comments were often heavily reinforced by other participants with nods and other positive body language and murmured agreement.

INCREASING POOR PEOPLE'S OPPORTUNITIES TO PARTICIPATE

Most people who participated in the project had not been involved in such debates before and had had few opportunities to develop their thoughts and ideas about poverty. It was therefore important to provide clear, jargon-free information and explain what we were doing fully to people, to meet the concern that all should have the support they needed to participate. In the event, everyone who took part was able to contribute.

In many ways this was a pilot project. This kind of research takes time and requires considerable sensitivity and skill. We were not able to include all the groups we would have liked, because of the difficulties we experienced reaching them. Participatory research has particular resource implications to ensure that all participants are able to take part on a positive and equal footing, without being out of pocket. We were learning as we went along, as were some of the anti-poverty organisations who put us in touch with the groups who took part in the project. The lesson we have learned is that it can be done and we hope that this will be only the first of many efforts to include people with experience of poverty fully in anti-poverty research and debates.

NOTES

1 C Oppenheim and L Harker, *Poverty: the facts,* Revised and updated third edition, CPAG, 1996.
2 P Wilding, *Introduction,* in Campaign Against Poverty, Decade of Despair, Campaign Against Poverty, 1989.

3 B Holman, *Shaken But Not Heard*, Guardian, 22 January 1994; S Croft and P Beresford, *The Lobby That Leads Nowhere*, Guardian, 14 December 1988.

4 P Beresford and S Croft, *It's Our Problem Too!: Challenging the exclusion of poor people from poverty discourse*, Critical Social Policy Issue 44/45, Autumn 1993, pp75-95.

5 P Hoggett and D Burns, *The Revenge of the Poor: The anti-poll tax campaign in Britain*, Critical Social Policy Issue 33, Winter 1991/92, pp95-110.

6 R Lister, *The Child Support Act: Shifting family financial obligations in the United Kingdom*, Social Politics, Issue 2, Summer 1994, pp211-221.

7 S Wilkinson and C Kitzinger, *Representing the Other*, Sage, 1996

8 R Levitas, *The Concept of Social Exclusion and the New Durkheimian Hegemony*, Critical Social Policy, Volume 16 (1), February 1996, pp5-20.

9 M Oliver, *Understanding Disability: From theory to practice*, Macmillan, 1996; J Morris (editor), *Encounters with Strangers: Feminism and disability*, The Women's Press, 1996.

10 D Hevey, *The Creatures that Time Forgot: Photography and disability imagery*, Routledge, 1992.

11 J Morris, *Independent Lives?: Community care and disabled people*, Macmillan, 1993; M Oliver, *Understanding Disability: From theory to practice*, Macmillan, 1996; J Campbell and M Oliver, Disability Politics: Understanding our past, changing our future, Routledge, 1996.

12 D Vincent, *Poor Citizens*, Longman, 1991.

13 H Rose, *Up Against the Welfare State: The claimant unions*, in R Miliband and J Saville (editors), The Socialist Register, Merlin, 1973.

14 D R Marshall, *The Politics of Participation in Poverty: A case study of the economic and youth opportunities agency of greater Los Angeles*, University of California Press, 1971.

15 *Fundamental Principles of Disability*, The Union of the Physically Impaired Against Segregation and the Disability Alliance, 1976.

16 S Croft and P Beresford, *Involving the Poor in Poverty Research*, Benefits Research, The Bulletin of the Social Fund Project, Issue 5, 1990, pp20-23.

17 S Croft, *Sharing the Wider Issues of Poverty*, Social Work Today, 16 February 1989, p39.

18 R Lister and P Beresford, *Working Together Against Poverty: Involving poor people in action against poverty*, Open Services Project and Department of Applied Social Studies, University of Bradford, 1991.

19 ATD Fourth World, *The Wresinski Approach: The poorest partners in democracy*, 1991; ATD Fourth World, *Talk With Us Not At Us: How to develop partnerships between families in poverty and professionals*, 1996; See also Fourth World Journal: The newsletter of ATD Fourth World

20 Church Action on Poverty, *London Poverty Hearing*, Church Action on Poverty, London and Manchester, 1995; F Bennett, *Local People National Voice: Speaking from experience*, Policy Group Report, Church Action on Poverty, 1996.

21 H Russell (editor), *Speaking from Experience: Voices at the National Poverty Hearing*, Church Action on Poverty, 1996.

22 F Bennett, *Local People National Voice: Speaking from experience*, Policy Group Report, Church Action on Poverty, 1996.

23 P Beresford and M Turner, *It's Our Welfare: Report of the Citizens' Commission on the Future of the Welfare State*, National Institute for Social Work, 1996.

24 UK Coalition Against Poverty, Participation Sub-Group, *Poverty and Participation: Learnings from a September 1996 workshop bringing together people living in poverty throughout the UK*, UK Coalition Against Poverty, 1997.

25 L A Singh (editor), *The UKCAP Eradicate Poverty Resource Pack*, UK Coalition Against Poverty, 1997.

26 P Holford, *Community Action Against Poverty*, Poverty, CPAG, 1997, pp4-6.

27 Local Government Anti-Poverty Unit, *Partners in Practice: Good practice in partnership for anti-poverty*, Anti-Poverty Matters, Issue 7, Winter 1995, pp8-9.

28 The Scottish Anti-Poverty Network, *The Scottish Declaration on Poverty: A framework for action against poverty by central and local government, health boards, enterprise companies and the private, voluntary and community sectors*, the Scottish Anti-Poverty Network, 1996.

29 P Townsend, *Poverty in the United Kingdom*, Penguin, 1979; J Mack and S Lansley, *Poor Britain*, George Allen and Unwin, 1985.

30 For example, R Cohen, J Coxall, G Craig, A Sadiq-Sangster, *Hardship Britain: Being poor in the 1990s*, CPAG, 1992; S Middleton, K Ashworth and R Walker, *Family Fortunes: Pressures on parents and children in the 1990s*, CPAG, 1994.

31 For example, A Shaw, K Kellard, R Walker, *Barriers, Bridges and Behaviour: Learning from income support recipients*, In-house report 18, Social Research Branch, Department of Social Security, 1996.

32 For example, E Kempson, *Life on a Low Income*, Joseph Rowntree Press, 1996.

33 B Jordan, *A Theory of Poverty and Exclusion*, Polity Press, 1996.

34 S Becker, *Responding to Poverty: The politics of cash and care*, Longman, 1997.

35 M Oliver, *The Politics of Disablement*, Macmillan, 1990, pp8-9; J Morris, *Pride Against Prejudice*, The Women's Press, 1991, pp130-133.

36 A Stanton, *Invitation to Self-Managment*, Dab Hand Press, 1989; P Beresford, *Researching Citizen Involvement: A collaborative or colonising enterprise?*, in M Barnes and G Wistow, Researching User Involvement, The Nuffield Institute for Health Services Studies, 1992; M Oliver, *Understanding Disability: From theory to practice*, Macmillan, 1996.

37 A Stanton, *Invitation to Self-Managment*, Dab Hand Press, 1989, p332.

38 P Beresford and J Cambell, *Disabled People, Service Users, User Involvement and Representation*, Disability and Society, Vol 9, No 3, 1994, pp315-325.

39 H Kettleborough, *Consulting Women in the Community about Local Government Services,* Critical Social Policy, No 12, 1988, pp56-67; and note 38.

Part Two

WHAT POOR PEOPLE SAY

INTRODUCTION

In part two of the book we move from the world of books, reports and media and political pronouncements on poverty to the worlds of people with experience of poverty themselves.

The second phase of this project took us from libraries, book shelves, press cuttings and video recordings, to making contact with, meeting, talking and working with people with experience of poverty themselves. For us this has been the most exciting and challenging part of the project. It marks the move from dealing with data to working *with* people, which is at the heart of the project's philosophy. The difficulties which we experienced in reaching and involving poor people also highlight the isolation which many face.

The world of poor people is not just one of deprived inner and outer city estates in run-down regions. Poverty in the UK exists in north and south and rich and poor areas; in genteel suburbs and idyllic rural settings.[1] It affects respectable old and disrespectful young; people conventionally included as middle class as well as working class. The discussions that make up this project included all these groups and situations.

We met people in well resourced centres with modern furniture and equipment; lively projects, bristling with notices for new activities and events; dreary offices and under-resourced meeting rooms, available free for meetings with tatty chairs and tables, and in cosy front rooms with cups of tea and biscuits. The rooms in which discussions were held, were sometimes cold and dark, with uncomfortable seats; sometimes warm, homely and inviting. Discussions were noisy, eventful, emotional and passionate, with people repeatedly saying that this was the first time they had ever had a chance to talk about these things.

Discussions were sometimes also hurried and interrupted. The many and varied demands on women were particularly in evidence; whether it was looking after children or partners, going shopping or running errands, rather than having time of their own. The audio tapes tell the story, with people's words interspersed with babies' cries and children's voices and the scraping of chairs and hasty apologies marking participants' comings and goings.

It is very difficult to do justice to the hundreds of thousands of words that make up people's discussions. We have had to leave out more than we could include and it is difficult on the printed page to give more than a hint of the feelings, emotions and experience of the many people who took part in the project.

Here people speak for themselves. We have tried to keep our comments to the minimum and avoid offering any interpretations of our own.

NOTES

1   C Philo (editor), *Off the Map: The social geography of poverty in the UK*, CPAG, 1995.

3 Defining and talking about poverty

WHAT IS POVERTY?

The definition of poverty has been one of the sticking points in discussions about poverty. As we have seen, while academic and pressure group debates about definition increasingly reflect the complexity and value-based nature of the subject, political discussions have long been polarised between what are presented as conflicting and opposed absolute and relative ideas of poverty. We wanted people with direct experience of poverty to have an opportunity to voice their thoughts and views on its definition and conceptualisation, and to do this in an arena where they would be taken seriously and could become part of the broader debate. We first asked participants their opinions of conventional definitions of poverty and then asked them how they would define it themselves.

CONVENTIONAL DEFINITIONS OF POVERTY

To find out participants' thoughts and ideas about the conventional definition of poverty, we asked them their views of the three definitions of poverty used in the British Social Attitudes Survey. This makes it possible to relate the views of people with direct experience of poverty to broader discussions about poverty definition. We read out the three definitions in order to each group. The definitions are progressively more absolute. Below are the quantified responses of participating groups followed with a comparison with the general population. Clearly the numbers do not permit detailed analysis, but they give an helpful idea of the distribution of views in the project. Of the 20 groups taking part 18 were asked and answered the question.

DEFINITION ONE

Would you say that someone in Britain was or was not poor if they had enough to buy the things they really needed but not enough to buy the things that most people take for granted?

Eight of the groups agreed unanimously that this defined poverty; six were undecided; and four of the groups unanimously disagreed with this definition of poverty.

DEFINITION TWO

Would you say that someone in Britain was or was not poor if they had enough to eat and live but not enough to buy other things they needed?

Thirteen of the groups unanimously agreed that this defined poverty; four were undecided; and one unanimously disagreed with this definition.

DEFINITION THREE

Would you say that someone in Britain was or was not poor if they had not enough to eat and live without getting into debt?

All 18 groups asked unanimously agreed that this defined poverty.

TABLE 1: **Public definitions of poverty**			
% would say someone in Britain was in poverty if ...	1986	1989	1994
they had enough to buy the things they really needed, but not enough to buy the things most people take for granted	25	25	28
they had enough to eat and live, but not enough to buy other things they needed	55	60	60
they had not got enough to eat and live without getting into debt	95	95	90

Reproduced from *British Social Attitudes*, 1995

While we can see that there is some variation in the responses of groups to these different definitions, it is also apparent that the definition of poverty which people were most able to agree with is the narrowest, most absolute one. However there was a slightly greater tendency among participants over the general population to view the most relative definition, definition one, as also describing poverty. Participants also talked in more detail about the definitions, raising a number of issues:

DEFINITION ONE: WHAT ARE NECESSITIES?

There was debate between participants around which items constitute necessities and which luxuries. Many who thought that the first definition did define poverty, considered that items generally believed to be luxuries, such as designer trainers, were in fact necessities:

> The things you need: food, electricity, gas, water; but you've got many people who take for granted a fridge, you need fuel in winter, you can't afford to go out and buy two bags of coal, you can't afford to have the electric fire on because your heating bill's sky high. Your kids want trainers, they'll not wear cheap trainers. You get them cheap trainers they're just left in the lobby hall – they'll not wear them. So you've got to go for a name, that's how kids pick on them at school. I mean that's more of an essential than a luxury. There's nowt as cruel as kids is there? I mean they that get free clothing, you can tell. So you have to go out and buy a uniform and then while they're wearing that one you've got to save up to get another one because it's changing. But these are essentials but people don't see them as essentials. (Group of unemployed people, Yorkshire)

As can be seen from the following discussion, some participants felt that it was difficult to determine what is a necessity as it is highly subjective:

> Most people you will find who are on benefits will have kids with one pair of shoes, that's what my kids have, one pair of wellies, that's it.
>
> One set of shoes.
>
> Well do they need more than one pair?
>
> No, probably not.
>
> When you weren't poor would your children have had more than one pair of shoes each?

Um, no.

No, maybe they wouldn't. Well they might have a ...

How do you differ what's needed and what's not? (LETS group)

The dilemma of what is a necessity and what a luxury was picked up in other discussions. These Glasgow lone parents, for example, debated whether a car was a luxury or a necessity:

It depends what other people take for granted.

Yes, some people take for granted having a car.

I would say that that was a necessity.

For some, DSS grants and loans do not go far enough in the provision of necessities:

You can get loans can't you but then they take all your money don't they? With babies they say it is essential for a fridge to keep a bottle of milk fresh but over a certain age they can do without a fridge. A cooker's essential. (Group of unemployed people, Yorkshire)

Others felt that if poor people were perceived by others to possess goods seen by some to be luxury items, such as electrical goods, that they would be criticised. Many participants did not see the possession of a television as a luxury:

I must say with the first one [definition], it makes me think. This woman who I was having an argument with, she said, 'Well, like, you've all got TVs in your home and I didn't have a TV or something', but she would go on holidays abroad or whatever. She was talking about working class people saying that, like, we don't work hard enough and we're just sitting there with our TVs and videos and all those sorts of things and it's like she was counting a TV as a luxury but it's not a luxury. I mean if you didn't rent or buy the second hand TV it's not like you'd then have the money to have a decent diet for the rest of your life. (Women's group)

A minority of participants felt that if an individual possesses all of the necessities for life then he or she could not be classified as poor:

So you can buy everything you need ... I wouldn't class that as being poor if you can buy everything that you need. (Members of a young people's project)

Well, the first one sounds to me as though people are managing quite nicely and just couldn't afford the luxuries which you don't need anyway. (Group of unemployed people, London)

These participants equated 'poverty' with bare subsistence:

Enough to put food on the table – no that isn't really poor.

Just getting by, that's what it is, from day to day, week to week. Getting by and getting by and getting by. (Group of young people)

But some participants voiced the opinion that living with just necessities was dehumanising:

They dehumanise it if they assess the limit on so-called necessities, you need more than necessities to be human.

Oh, yes.

Yes, because you hope that you've got several years of life left when you retire and you just don't want to live in a straitjacket.

You want to be able to enjoy what you've worked for all your life.

That's what distinguishes a human being from an animal. For the animal all it needs possibly is sufficient to live, where humans need something else and they're being denied that. (Group of older people)

There's more to life than existing. Everybody's entitled to get something in their life. (Group of disabled people)

This participant argued that life without leisure constitutes poverty:

I think everybody needs some sort of leisure pursuits and if they've only got enough to pay for what they really need, for basic needs, I would say that was poor. (Community centre users group)

Others stressed the financial costs of any social contact:

Well the television isn't an absolute necessity providing you've got something to occupy your mind, but you must go out because if you stay in that causes severe depression – you must go out. And when I say go out, I don't mean socialise, spend so many pounds a night on luxury meals, I simply mean enough money to go out, meet your friends and just get yourself away from those four walls. (Group of unemployed people, London)

In this exchange, participants found it difficult to decide whether the first definition constituted poverty given the need of people in the Third World:

> I'd say it was borderline poverty.

> Well people have different ideas about what's needed.

> I mean, like, a poor person in Africa would set their standards ...

> We can't worry about Africa – let's worry about our problems.

> No, I'm saying there's different standards of what's needed, isn't there? We want a decent house, a bit of shopping and decent clothes. We want that and we can only just afford to get that sometimes. (Lone parent's group, Yorkshire)

DEFINITION TWO: QUALITY OF LIFE

Again many of the discussions around this definition of poverty focused on the subjective nature of necessity. The majority of groups agreed that this definition did reflect poverty in Britain:

> I think that's poverty.

> Yes, that's poverty. If you haven't got things that you need. (Lone parent's group, Glasgow)

Some participants echoed the discussion around the first definition in focusing on the issue of quality of life. They thought that quality of life should be central to any definition of poverty:

> It's not just about food is it, it's about the mental aspect.

> The quality of your life.

> You've got to have quality life.

> Not just existing.

> It isn't existing. I mean we feed our animals but we feed them because we care for them and we're giving them a quality of life. In a lot of cases sometimes our dogs and cats are getting more protein than we are ourselves. (Women's education project)

For many participants discussing the second definition of poverty, quality of life centred around basic issues such as hygiene. These participants thought that benefits made no provision for anything that could be regarded as a quality life:

On benefits I don't think that any allowance is made for brushing your teeth or buying loo rolls or soap, or the odd bubble bath … Luxuries for people on benefits are 'Do I buy toothpaste this week or soap the next?'

Buy toilet rolls, toothpaste, scouring powder, washing powder, washing up liquid and you can double just what you pay for your food bill. Quite happily you can double the amount needed to live today if you are worried about such things as keeping your house clean, keeping your clothes clean. (LETS group)

This participant argued that people can sacrifice many of the things they perceive as being necessities and still lead quality lives:

I think if you cut down on things like drinking and smoking and you have the bare necessities of life; or like if you can only have a full meal a day with a shelter over your head and you had clothing then basically you don't need a great deal. (Member of Mental health service users group)

DEFINITION THREE: ABSOLUTE POVERTY IN BRITAIN

Many participants, including this member of a community centre users group, observed that the definitions presented became progressively more absolute, with this third definition summing up absolute poverty in Britain:

I think we would agree that all of those people are poor, but in each quote they seem to be poorer and poorer – but I think they're all poor, but getting poorer the more you're talking about them.

There was a consensus that the third definition gave a much more desperate depiction of poverty than the first two:

I think the third one because if you can't afford to eat and live then you are classed as poor really. I mean if you've got enough to eat and live, you're still surviving. (Members of a group for low income families)

These participants thought that the third definition characterised the lives of many single parents:

That's chronic poverty … Yes, I think most single parents are living in chronic poverty. (Member of lone parent's group, Glasgow)

They are all poverty but the last one is what you'd call poverty. I mean if you've got enough money to buy food and the things you need but not the things most people take for granted …

You have enough to eat and live but not enough to buy other things you need.

But what we're saying is sometimes we don't have enough to buy the things we need because, as you said, we get to the check-out and find out we have to put half the stuff back, and the stuff that is really essential. (Group of lone parents, Bristol)

A lone parent argued that the absolute poverty captured in the third definition is now commonplace in contemporary Britain but it has many parallels with what we associate with 'Dickensian' poverty:

I think that people equate poverty now with Dickens' times, you know, the absolute grinding poverty. And yet in some ways if you equate what we've got it's not so different. I mean I did a course at college in history and going back to the Poor Law in the 1500s and you're basically reading the same as what we are now on the policy thing and that. It's that sort of a nightmare, it's never ever going to change. If it's not changed in that time it's never ever going to change. (Group of lone parents, Yorkshire)

POVERTY, DEBT AND CREDIT

The third definition prompted a discussion of debt and the ways in which many loan companies encourage people to take out easy-payment options. This member of a mental health service users' group argued that people need not get into debt:

Oh, I think when people get into debt they're really reckless.

A large majority of participants however thought that debt characterised the lives of many poor people in Britain. 'Easy-payment' options, available through many catalogues, were thought to encourage many people into debt:

I'm not sure how people do manage to eat and survive in Britain without getting into some sort of debt, albeit for children's catalogues, you can pay cheaply over obviously spreading costs over a number of weeks, that is an option, but you are still getting into debt. (LETS group)

Well, what that lady said earlier about catalogues and getting their clothes from catalogues. I think you'll find that the vast majority of people in _____ [Glasgow estate] use catalogues or Provident cheques, or shopper's cheques rather than having the cash to go out and buy what they need. They need to get into debt because they

can't afford to buy what they need. (Members of a community centre
users group)

POVERTY AND THE THIRD WORLD

The discussion of absolute poverty prompted by the third definition
led many groups to make comparisons between poverty in Britain
and poverty in many Third World countries. Although it was
recognised that poverty existed in Britain, the absolute poverty of the
Third World was held to be of a completely different nature and
magnitude. Poverty in the Third World was held to be the benchmark
against which other, more relative poverties, should be judged:

> I mean that's what I would class as poor. Definitely because I mean
> people are actually dying because they're not getting enough food, or
> clothes or stuff like that, or even somewhere to live. So that's poverty.
> I mean I wouldn't class having enough money just to feed yourself,
> that's short of money. (A member of a Group for low income families)

> I mean when you come in, look emaciated, weigh about five stone, no
> clothes and no food, then I'll say you're really, really destitute and
> poor. You're not poor really, you're having a hard time – we're all
> having a hard time. If you want to see suffering you go to the third
> world and you'll soon come running back here. We're poor and it's
> not very nice, but to them, we've got luxuries. (Group of unemployed
> people, London)

> That's real poverty. They're living on grain and rice and shit – that's
> poverty, you know, what I mean. If we had to do that we would be
> really _____ upset. (Group of young people)

> But what I'm saying is that if you're finding people who are in a
> position like Ethiopia, somewhere like that, and they have no food,
> virtually no clothes and they are nearly starving, obviously they are
> poor. If you have then, higher up the social scale maybe even at the
> top of the local scale, people who have a fair degree of clothing, a
> certain amount of food – but probably not enough – but they'd be
> much worse off than you because they won't have a house, they won't
> have electric light, they won't have shoes for example. Are the people
> at the top of that scale still poor, or are they better off than poor, even
> though they're poorer than you? (Rural tenants group)

Some participants felt rich in comparison to people in Third World countries:

> I don't think any of us are in poverty and any of us have ever been in poverty.

> We're not in a Third World country, we're just not well-off.

> I mean compared to them we've got it rather cushy but compared to other people in this country, we're like we're the Third World to them. (Group of young people)

Others argued that a difference between people in relative poverty in Britain and in absolute poverty in Third World countries was the opportunity, however limited, for people in Britain to break-free of poverty:

> Yes, but they're poor, they're in poor countries. We're not in a poor country, we're in a pretty rich country.

> That's right. So we have the ability to get out of this. (Group of disabled people)

These members of a LETS group felt that people in relative poverty in Britain realised that the suffering experienced by poor people in the Third World was of a different type and magnitude to their own and were sympathetic to their cause:

> It's different in India. I really have seen poverty and I've seen myself in India some really, really, really ... poverty where nobody would care at all.

> And I imagine there's not many people on benefits who can go past a Rwanda appeal and not put 10p in because you know there are people out there who are really suffering.

However, one homeless person saw the comparison between Britain and the Third World as an attempt to marginalise further the problem of absolute poverty in Britain:

> That's another example of how some people think and then ignore the plight of people in this country, well, it's nothing compared with the situation like that. They can get away with the fact that what you are complaining about: Look at those poor people. And even within this country where there isn't a war situation or anything like that there's people begging, people who have got nothing.

One group felt that, although materially poorer, third world countries often perceived richer nations to be spiritually poor:

> In poverty-stricken countries they look at the western world as in some ways poor. They think we're mentally impoverished, spiritually impoverished.

> Yes, that's right, they look on the western world as spiritually impoverished. A lot of those countries they feel sorry for a lot of people in the western world. (Mental health service users' group)

PEOPLE'S OWN DEFINITIONS OF POVERTY

We wanted participants to have the chance to offer their own definitions of poverty as well as commenting on existing ones. Most participants had the chance to do this in response to the question, 'How would you define the word "poverty"?', although sometimes people offered comments in other parts of the discussions. Although some participants had difficulty with this question and many took time to think, most were able to offer their own definitions. While it was something that they may not have been asked before, or perhaps have thought about, it was certainly an issue on which they had views to offer. This section includes the whole range of responses participants put forward, which fall into three categories. These are:

- financially and materially based definitions;
- restricted behaviour based definitions;
- psychologically and spiritually based definitions.

FINANCIALLY AND MATERIALLY BASED DEFINITIONS OF POVERTY

These include definitions offered by participants where they used some kind of purely material deficiency to classify people as being in poverty. The majority of personal definitions people gave fitted into this category. For example:

> Well not having enough income so that you can have a reasonable quality of life.

> And what kind of things do you include as reasonable?

> Sufficient for clothing. (A member of a group for low income families in conversation with the project worker)

Other comments reflected the same emphasis:

> I think poverty is where you've got no money and you feel it's for no purpose and you can't see any way out of it. During the year we were poor and we were poor because I had two single lads who'd got nothing and we all lived on thirty quid which was my income support. (Women's education project)

> Not being able to buy what you want for the kids and that. (Group of unemployed people, Yorkshire)

> Not being able to meet the mortgage and the bills or the rates. (Group of unemployed people, London)

> Not having enough to eat. (Young people's project)

> The people that are really poor, I'd say, are the people that haven't got the means to get what they need. As long as people have got means … as long as they've got means of getting, of surviving, whatever way they do it, apart from breaking the law that is, then it's not too bad. (Mental health service users group)

> When you live week by week you're poor and being poor is just not having enough to pay for what you need for that week, everything that you'll need bills, food, clothes. If you haven't got enough for that then you're poor. (Lone parent's group, Yorkshire)

> I think surely the blanket term for poverty in England today has got to be can you go home, have you got a home to go to, have you got a roof over your house, have you got food for the night, reasonable warmth and clothing to get you through another day isn't it? I know we have but statistically I guess there are people out there who really probably don't. (LETS group)

> Poverty to me is not having the basic things that you need like a car if you're employed, or a home, and an adequate fired house that is dry and reasonably furnished … that's this Government's attitude that you should be able to work for Third World wages and still be able to pay your fuel costs. And then they wonder why the house is riddled with damp. I think in all honesty if you need a car to get to work it's a necessity. You need adequate shelter and according to the housing legislation that is overall governed by central government, you should have room for the ages of the kids living in that household. (Member of lone parent's group, Glasgow)

Even simple things like 'apologising for having a decent lawnmower' was regarded by these participants as a definition of poverty:

> Well I am insured, but the thing is the lawnmower was stolen and I've got a nice garden, I love my garden, and my luxury was a nice lawnmower and I had it stolen ...

> You shouldn't be apologising for having a decent lawnmower. Put that down, that's poverty, apologising for having a decent lawnmower.

> ... apologising, yes, because that was my luxury. Having a decent lawnmower. Yes it was stolen but the insurance company won't pay out until you've been and bought another one and actually got a receipt for it. Where the heck do you go and get your money to go and buy a decent lawnmower? (Women's education project)

One participant distinguished between different degrees of poverty:

> Poverty is somebody that's not got a lot of things and there's no hope for them. I mean some people you class as 'poverty stricken' wouldn't see themselves as poverty stricken because they've got enough to get by with and there's always a light at the end of the tunnel, that one of these days it might change. Then there's people that are absolutely poverty stricken, people that are that far down there's no way out. (Group for low income families)

RESTRICTED BEHAVIOUR BASED DEFINITIONS OF POVERTY

These were definitions put forward by participants where behaviours or choices were restricted in some way. As a result, they either cannot do what they want to do, or feel they should be able to do:

> Poverty for me is a certain lack of choice. I enrolled on a college course which had the fees paid for me. I could have continued on the course but I looked at my piece of paper and I worked out my expenses and I couldn't afford the bus fare in and out and I couldn't have afforded food so I could not go on that course, it would have meant five pounds out the purse. At the moment it is not viable for me to do it. Maybe in the future I can think of going back to college but not at the moment. And that is poverty I think, not to be able to better myself. (LETS group)

> I would define poverty as not being able to do the things that you want to do in life. (Group of unemployed people, London)

I class myself as poor when I've got to avoid the charity box that I'd want to put in. (Group of disabled people)

Having to go out and having to apologise for not being able to pay my way in a group or even representing the Centre. Maybe I might go out, I might get the money back afterwards but I'd have to lay money out before hand, so I'm sat there counting the money in my pocket wondering if I can afford to pay for what I've got to pay for. (Lone parent's group, Yorkshire)

Poverty, for this homeless participant, was defined in terms of not being able to pursue the type of lifestyle which was perceived to be followed by most people in a given society – a relative deprivation model:

I would define it in terms of being unable for financial reasons to follow the sort of lifestyle which you could feel reasonably be expected to be followed by the majority of people. (Group of homeless people)

PSYCHOLOGICALLY AND SPIRITUALLY BASED DEFINITIONS OF POVERTY

This was the category of personal definitions that was most unlike conventional poverty definitions. In these definitions participants associated poverty with a particular psychological or spiritual state. These two groups argued that poverty is a psychological or spiritual state unrelated to an individual's financial situation:

I think that poverty is like a state of mind really and if someone is really in a state of poverty, then it's not that difficult to define.

Poverty is a state of mind because on the one hand you can have very rich people who still fell inadequate about themselves, about the fact that they don't have certain things in life and they still feel they're not happy in life, so they still feel poverty of thought, poverty of knowledge and poverty of spirit. (Mental health service users' group)

You're poor if you're poor in spirit even if you have millions and many people are poor in spirit because with the millions they've got, they haven't got the brains or the spirit to do something helpful with the money they've got. (Group of older people)

DO PARTICIPANTS SEE THEMSELVES AS POOR?:

We have now presented both the ideas of participants about conventional definitions of poverty and their own personal conceptions. As we will see in Chapter 5, participants related personal experiences of often extreme poverty, by conventional definitions. Yet paradoxically many of the same participants, when discussing the definition of poverty, did not perceive themselves, or wish to be perceived, as being poor. The reasons for this seem complex. There has been some discussion in conventional analysis of poverty, of people's reluctance to acknowledge their poverty because of the stigma and condemnation associated with it. It is to be expected that this influenced some of the people who took part in the project. But what emerged much more strongly from the people we spoke to and seemed to underpin their comments, was the sense that there were other people in much more constrained circumstances than them and it was they who were really in poverty. This connects with the comments they made about poverty and the Third World which exemplified the notion of 'relative deprivation'. Of course, this could, itself, in turn reflect to some extent an unwillingness to identify with the label poverty. In addition comments were made such as:

No, not poverty. Hard up, yes, but not poverty. (Rural tenants group)

In an exchange between the project worker and a member of a young people's project, one member of the group said:

Well, I say that there's people worse off than what we are.

There's people worse, like who?

It could be anybody somewhere out there. Perhaps they do not get any money at all – they can't get money, they can't get a job.

A few participants, however, felt that they were relatively poor:

Well, I regard myself as poor compared to most in Britain, the majority of people in Britain ... I don't like complaining a great deal because I know full well that I've got food to eat and I can get by, but that's me. (Group of unemployed people, London)

THE LANGUAGE OF POVERTY

CONVENTIONAL TERMINOLOGY

We asked participants their views on terms used in conventional poverty discussions, words such as 'poor' and 'poverty'. Opinion was firmly divided concerning the value of these terms. This is where the issue of stigma was raised by participants. Some thought that these terms were stigmatising:

> Stigma. As soon as you mention 'poverty'. (Member of a group for low income families)

The term 'poverty' brought to mind a stigmatising portrait of destitution for many people:

> No I think it's a horrid word because I think straight away you conjure up this person sitting huddled in the cold. (LETS group)

This participant felt that the stigma attached to these terms makes poor people appear 'untrustworthy':

> It does label you, there's no question about it … If you are poor, shall we say, not as wealthy as some, you are considered to be worse in some ways, socially worse - you are literally socially worse, but even as a person, quality of character, it's automatically 'you're poor' therefore you steal or may steal. You're not worthy, you're untrustworthy. (Group of unemployed people, London)

An exchange between the project worker and a group of members of a young people's project demonstrates some of the difficulties with the word, poverty:

> It's a horrible word to use!
>
> *Why is it a horrible word to use?*
>
> Because it sounds really bad that.
>
> *What kind of word would you use?*
>
> I don't really know, but I wouldn't use that one.
>
> If you saw that word, would you think, Yes, I know all about that, that's me ! Or would you think, Oh, that's a shame? I'd think it was a shame.
>
> It puts you down.

It puts people down. Do you think it puts people down?

Yes, Yes.

So if somebody says that you were 'poverty-struck' you'd feel put down by it would you?

Well, I wouldn't, but a lot of people would. It depends on which way you look at it, doesn't it? If you're saying it to help you then it's different, but people say it just to get at you.

So, do you feel insulted in that sense?

Yes.

Conversely many participants thought that is necessary to highlight the plight of people in poverty:

Poverty is the word we want to use.

We are in poverty.

Poor. (Group of older people)

Because if you don't say what poverty is and call it poverty then it's going to be invisible. (Group of women involved in campaigns)

In this way, participants thought that the term 'poverty' rendered the invisible visible:

I think it's an eye-opener.

Well, it's helpful isn't it?

I think the more people who accept that they're living in poverty and talk about it openly, I think more people would start admitting that they're living in poverty. All this crap about 'Oh, I can manage'. (Women's education project)

Even where there was a feeling that conventional terminology was helpful, there was still confusion over the multiplicity of terms used in conventional poverty discussions, so, for example, in an exchange between the project worker, and a group of homeless people:

Do you think poverty is a helpful term now? Do you think it's a helpful term or do you think it's not one that we should use?

Well I've already said that it's useful to describe some people as being in 'poverty' but I think poor is another term for it.

Do you think that 'poor' is a better word than 'poverty'?

Not to describe people living on the streets and in squalid conditions, no, I think poverty is a much better term.

And you talked about destitution. Can you differentiate between poverty and destitution?

Only in relative terms really. Destitution is someone who is far worse off than someone in poverty.

Furthermore, as this lone parent from Bristol commented, the use of terms, such as these, are highly subjective anyway:

If you saw any of us walking down the street I think we're all fairly smart and we're all proud people so how would you know who's poor and who's not. To understand about poverty, poverty does not mean, like, scruffiness, it doesn't mean down at heel. We've all worked in the past, we've all worked part-time now and then or whatever, but you could have one person who is a lot better dressed than the next person. How do you define who's in poverty and who isn't. I don't think you can just use the word poverty if you haven't got a clue what you're talking about.

It doesn't matter what you do you're always going to split hairs with words like that. It's just a fashion, it's like manipulating figures for unemployment. If we say that we're doing this and doing that, it makes it look as if there's less and all you're saying is that if you look as if you're in a different grade. It's like us being snobbish in wanting to be classed a little better than being poor or being a beggar. (Group of lone parents, Yorkshire)

Despite this, participants felt that if a term could be universally agreed upon that describes poverty, without stigmatising poor people, then this could be used as a basis for empowerment:

If we can make it simple, I mean fair-dos, poverty is a kind of buzz word. People don't know the actual meaning of poverty, if you can get a wee buzz word, whether it be poor or whatever, I use it all the time but just some kind of wee statement or something like that – that will stick in people's minds. This is 'poverty'. They go to that picture of what poverty is and the different experiences it entails. If you can do that then we'll give people the understanding to enable them to empower themselves and take action and join together. It's a crazy ideal, but if it happens, it will make a big change. (Anti-poverty youth group)

ALTERNATIVE TERMINOLOGY

Due to the amount of ambiguity and stigma surrounding conventional poverty terminology and the significance that some participants seemed to attach to this, we specifically asked a small number of participants, where time permitted, if they had alternative terms to offer. These are some of the suggestions people made:

Social deprivation. (Anti-poverty youth group)

Just 'not well off' – poverty sounds terrible. (Members of a community centre users group)

'Hard up' – it's not the idea of poverty itself, it's 'not working'. It sounds better. (Members of a group for low income families)

What you could say really if you wanted to, sort of like, make it more pleasant is call it 'financially challenged'. (Group of unemployed people, London)

Financially disadvantaged if you want to be politically correct. (Group of older people)

Some terms seemed to be less objectionable to some people than others. But the key problem, seemed to be the category or problem of poverty itself. For one group at least, changing and challenging this was the issue:

Give the people a clear definition of what poverty really is ... Involve single parents, involve young homeless people ... If we don't pull our socks up and take action ... then poverty will continue, people will continue to be railroaded, the legislation to do with benefits, everything that poverty involves. (Anti-poverty youth group)

SUMMARY

CONVENTIONAL DEFINITIONS OF POVERTY

While some participants were undecided and there was a fair degree of support for more relative definitions of poverty, the conventional definition of poverty which all groups subscribed to was the most absolute definition. This was framed in terms of people not having 'enough to eat and live without getting into debt'.

POVERTY AND THE THIRD WORLD

Most participants thought that the absolute poverty encountered in the Third World was of a different kind and magnitude to the relative poverty identified in Britain. Many participants thought that this absolute poverty was a benchmark against which other types of poverty, and poverty elsewhere, should be judged.

PARTICIPANTS' OWN DEFINITIONS OF POVERTY

People's own definitions fell into three main categories. These were:

• financially and materially based definitions;
• restricted behaviour based definitions;
• psychologically and spiritually based definitions.

THE LANGUAGE OF POVERTY

Opinion was divided as to whether conventional poverty terminology was stigmatising. Some participants thought that it was, others believed words like 'poverty' and 'poor' to be valuable as they highlighted the severe problems many people in poverty experience. When asked, however, few of those asked could come up with alternative terms for 'poor' and 'poverty'.

4
The causes of poverty

In the discussion groups, we asked people for their thoughts about the causes of poverty. We asked people two questions: 'Why do you think people are poor?' and 'Do you think there are differences for different individuals and/or groups?' Participants found the second question difficult to answer and most comments were restricted to mentioning particular groups, like students, disabled people and lone parents. However participants had a lot to say about the first question. It was something they were eager to talk about and which they sometimes returned to in other parts of the discussions.

People's comments fell into two main categories, relating to *structural* and 'individualistic' (*non-structural*) explanations of poverty. One of the long-standing discussions in traditional poverty debate has been about whether poverty is caused by structural forces in society; broader processes and institutions, which push some people into poverty and keep them there, or by individuals themselves, through what is called their own *agency*. This structure/agency debate, as it has become known, is one of the main sticking points preventing people from agreeing about what causes poverty. The *right* tends to blame individuals for getting themselves into poverty, while critics of this position focus on structural causes. Participants in this project overwhelmingly put forward structural explanations of poverty. They did not, however, lose sight of their own agency in dealing with poverty, a theme which is beginning to emerge among some academics who subscribe to structural explanations. One or two deviated from structural explanations and these views are presented first.

NON-STRUCTURAL EXPLANATIONS OF POVERTY

This participant, for example, saw people living in poverty more as victims of chance, than subject to structural forces:

It's circumstances basically. Our poverty is nothing to do with where we were born, how we were born, whether we were born into working class backgrounds, middle class backgrounds, whatever. We're still relatively well educated people. We speak in a certain way, but it's circumstances that have made us poor. (LETS group)

He emphasised the importance of educational qualifications in finding work. Other participants talked about qualifications in terms of structure, but one young person saw the issue more in terms of agency, about how 'people ____ about at school':

You haven't got the qualifications to get the job so you're _____. A lot of people ____ around at school like everyone probably here used to ____ around at school. You know you leave school with ____ all and just from leaving school you go straight into signing on and then that's it. (Group of young people)

A woman in another group offers an example of how some participants combined structural and non-structural explanations. She talked about the way an educational and qualification "trap" perpetuated inter-generational poverty:

Poverty puts people in these little tiny traps. They can't really get out because if they're poor they're more likely to go to the school that doesn't care or put them in the back seat to sit down and so therefore they're not interested in what goes on in the community and the school or anything. They come out, they don't have enough 'O' or 'A' levels. They would not get a job and because they would not get a job, there they are, they are trapped in poverty. Then they start to get kids and the kids grow up in the same poverty, and then you go through the whole cycle again. the poverty, the deprivation, they all go together and they get mixed up. (Women's discussion group)

One mental health service user argued that an individual's desire for material goods, coupled with people leaving their family unit, were causes of poverty:

People should look at themselves and say, 'Am I poor because my material desires are constantly increasing?' So I'm trying to stay up with the Joneses and say, well should I try and get a fridge or a dishwasher or a cooker or a car or a computer? I mean all these material goods are there and people think they should have them because other people have them ... A lot of poverty occurs because people, when they split up from the family quite often are forced to start making a living for themselves. And when you do you have to start paying your own rent, your own telephone bills, electricity, gas, water, poll tax ... Staying within the family unit causes its own problems but certainly poverty is something that could be counter-acted by staying within that unit and staying together because you're sharing ... I think a lot of poverty stems from the fragmentation of the family unit. (Mental health service user's group)

STRUCTURAL EXPLANATIONS OF POVERTY

Most participants, however, saw the causes of poverty in structural terms. These fell into five broad categories, the first two of which in particular clearly overlap. We have retained the distinction between the two which participants drew in their comments. General government policy and specific anti-poverty policy were both seen to play a major part in contributing to the problem. The categories are:

- Unemployment and low paid employment;
- Politico-economic;
- General government policy;
- Government social security policy;
- More general social policies and issues.

We will now look at each of these in turn.

UNEMPLOYMENT AND LOW-PAID EMPLOYMENT

The majority of participants thought that unemployment was a major cause of poverty in the UK. Most comments about the issue, however, were monosyllabic and left undeveloped in the discussions. Typically when they were asked what caused poverty participants would say, 'unemployment' and others would nod and agree as if to say that this went without saying:

I think it's the unemployment isn't it. That's the biggest thing, unemployment. There's no work in Scotland. (Community centre users group)

Some participants who did develop this idea, talked about the closure of heavy industry, particularly in areas which depended on that one industry for people's livelihoods:

> People are expected to earn a living where there aren't jobs for them to do. I mean all right going out looking for jobs if there are jobs to be done, but the shipyards they've shut them all. The pits, they've shut them all. What are they going to do with all these men? (Women's education project)

An unemployed man from Yorkshire talked about the difficulties of moving to find work in less depressed areas:

> When all these pits shut 'round here, there were men coming out crying because they knew they'll never get another job. As for getting on your bike and finding work somewhere else, where are you going to get housing from? Where are you going to move your family to? What's your family going to do while you're not here? If you go down South, whatever you earn you'd have to pay rent. There'd be nothing to send home to your family. I think everything changes, everything.

Another unemployed person emphasised that even in some areas of 'the affluent South' work was hard to come by:

> I moved down to this area which seems much worse than Hornchurch. I did actually find little jobs when I was living there but I've found nothing since I've been living here and I tried for a year then went on a course. But people do think you're not trying, they believe there's work out there. (Group of unemployed people, London)

A number of participants emphasised the importance of education. The possession of educational qualifications was seen as vital in securing employment. This participant, however, argued that even qualifications were no guarantee of getting employment:

> I got my highers but I can't get a job anywhere. (Community centre users group)

But as one young man said, even if you could get employment, many jobs were no better than having to rely on benefits:

> Even if they do get a job it's usually like pretty shit and no better than the dole in the long run. (Group of young people)

At the time when some of the discussions took place there were tabloid reports of 'slave labour', including one where workers were being paid the equivalent of one pound an hour. Such reports appeared to strengthen the argument about low wages for participants:

> But what about people who are employed and they're only employed for twelve hours a week and they only get paid a pound an hour?

> Oh, I would take these folk to court. That's slave labour, that, being asked to work for a pound an hour.

> There was a case in the paper the other day of a shop paying somebody a pound an hour to work there.

> Now that's where you come down to where you're poor. That's when you come down to the crash-line. When you're poor, you'll do anything for money and that's what all these people are doing just to keep their head above water. (Community centre users group)

> You look at basic shop workers they're lucky to get £3.50 an hour. If you're cleaning you get bloody £2 ... A supermarket recently opened a development with the backing of the councillors. They said at a public meeting that they were creating 400 jobs, most part-time ... Some of these part-time workers are working eight and a quarter hours a week. I bet that 70% are working eight and a quarter hours a week. How much money do you earn doing that? That's a waste of bloody time even going to work. (A lone parent, Glasgow)

This participant believed that the abolition of the wages council coupled with the actions of employers had encouraged the growth of low paid work:

> We've lost the wages council, full-time working has been transferred into part-time temporary working and flexible hours being brought in ... They can employ thousands of people on their books. Now these people go to work places where in my case the going rate was five pounds an hour. These people were earning £2.50 an hour and doing exactly the same work but in many cases the management were going 'round saying there will be a job at the end of this, you keep your head down, you get working on, we'll give you a job. There was no job, there never was going to be a job, but they kept them thinking there was a job. (Women's education project)

POLITICO-ECONOMIC CAUSES

Some participants identified much broader causes to which they related unemployment; some seeing politico-economic causes of poverty in terms of the adverse effects of capitalism. Four groups saw poverty as having its roots in the wider economic and political framework of the market. A member of an anti-poverty youth group, for example, in conversation with the project worker said:

It's capitalism.

So what you're saying is that it's the whole economic sphere of capitalism that causes poverty?

Well it's the establishment being in existence and having control over everyday lives and what we do. We've got a certain amount of freedom but it's just down to the power of money. If you haven't got the power of money to do the things that you want to do, you can't.

A member of a women's education project said:

Capitalist system, that's what causes poverty. In a country where everybody's got their own little bit of land and can go out and do something about their situation there's not the poverty ... You stick somebody in a high-rise block of flats with three kids, they can do nothing about their situation, they have got to go out with their hand out and they have got no manoeuvring room ... there's a hierarchical structure and people are expected to know their place and not rise above it.

Discussing market economies, this participant argued that low waged labour is a physical and ideological way of 'maintaining the system':

The economy needs low wage workers and then you're so tired at the end of the day, you're not going to be able to do anything to change your situation either, so that also helps. (Member of a group of women involved in campaigns)

A member of a women's group discussing unemployment in the UK argued that the global market economy exploited labour in third world countries and consequently was a cause of poverty here:

These clothes they're all made in Third World countries. They're all made abroad and they're brought into this country, cheapest labour that makes them and they're brought into this country and they're sold for the highest price, that's wrong for me.

A link was also made with inflation as a cause of poverty:

> Prices go up regularly, the prices of commodities but the income
> virtually stays the same even if its not actually reducing ... The cost of
> things was pegged just after the war and for some time, and then
> suddenly it began to insidiously creep along, things began to get a little
> more expensive, a penny, tuppence and so forth, and of course, people
> had to have an increase in their pay. The first idea, the first way of
> doing this was not a bad idea. Everybody got five pounds a week
> across the board whatever their rank or status and then somebody or
> other, whether it was trade unions or the Government, or whatever at
> the time, they suddenly had the idea that the best thing to do is have a
> percentage. Ever since that, things have got worse and the people who
> have the most are better off all the time, the differential widens all the
> time. (Group of older people)

GENERAL GOVERNMENT POLICY

Participants in the project saw government and its policies as a key
cause of poverty. Of the 20 groups who took part in the project 13
expressed the view, without prompting, that in some way or other
Conservative government policy had been a central cause of poverty.
This older person, for example, saw politicians as self-interested and
self-motivated:

> It's the same people who are earning thirty or seventy thousand
> pounds a year, an MP who gets thirty-one thousand pounds a year and
> expenses, a free car, why don't they get rid of that and give us poor
> pensioners something. We fought for this country. I was away from
> my wife for five blasted years!

A lone parent joked that if MPs were single mothers, the economy
would be in better shape:

> It's your Central Government. Your politicians being male and having
> no concept of how to budget. If they could budget properly for the
> whole country and spend money cost-effectively the way we do as
> single parents. (Group of lone parents, Glasgow)

People argued that governments were aware of poverty, but were not
motivated to take action against it:

> It's not because the government, regardless of its colour, is unaware of
> the problem it's because there is no incentive for them to change it.
> (Group of older people)

This member of a women's group believed that this indifference was rooted in the politics of class:

> The Government ... they're not interested in the working class, they're interested in the upper class.

People felt that changes in the benefit and taxation systems had further penalised poor people:

> The Government ... Everything they give you they take away. They say that they're going to give you five pounds extra for Income Support then they do something like put VAT on the gas so it takes away ten pounds, so you're five pounds worse off. (Group of lone parents, Bristol)

> You've got loads of things like tax on heating and things whereas the less money you get, the chances are the houses are less well insulated so you've got to use more energy so therefore you've got to end up paying more anyway because you can't afford double beds and you can't afford a decent house. (Rural tenants group)

The student loans system was criticised for the same reason:

> The students are in the same problem that when they get a loan to help them with their education they're not getting paid while they're in education but when they get a job the interest on their basic loan has gone up and they're in debt as they're starting their working career. (Group of disabled people)

Governments which have repeatedly condemned 'dependence', were seen as fostering it:

> If you're dependent on the state nowadays you can't help it. It's due to the Government closing all these pits down, closing all these businesses down, importing instead of buying British. I mean all these jobs are going and it's all through this Government. (Group of unemployed people, Yorkshire)

THE PRIVATISATION OF UTILITIES AND SERVICES

The privatisation of services and utilities which was advanced on grounds of increasing choice and efficiency, was seen as a further cause of poverty. This group of older people thought that the encroachment of the private sector, especially in health care, and the resulting increased costs were a cause of poverty:

Your prescriptions were free, your glasses were free, your teeth were free. This Government has put everything up, privatisation has killed this country. (Group of older people)

Large utility bills were also thought to impoverish people :

Large bills, paying bills. People haven't got the money. (Group of unemployed people, London)

Some participants perceived increases in domestic bills as a direct result of privatisation policies. For example:

What actually makes it worse is British Telecom, British Gas. They're allowed to jump up their prices. I don't know how I'll get through this Winter because my electricity bill is more than a quarter of my income a week. I have to pay my electricity and I can still only afford to heat one room in the house and I've got a three bedroom house. And I think it's pathetic. (Lone parent's group, Glasgow)

SOCIAL SECURITY POLICY

The social security system figured large in people's analysis of the causes of poverty. Eighteen groups, to a greater or lesser extent, thought that it was a major cause of poverty in the UK. Levels of benefit, benefit policy and the operation of the benefit system were all judged to be inadequate.

A large number of participants, like this member of a group for low income families, believed that benefits were too low:

Social Security not giving you enough money!

Home owners who became claimants were thought to be especially vulnerable to poverty:

And it's worse because I own my own property and if I went back to Income Support ... Income Support does not pay the insurance on my property and I have to find £300 a year to pay that ... They think it's wonderful to own your property but it isn't and you have to pay most of the repairs − but now I'm having help with the repairs, I didn't know this before. So you're living well below the bread-line because you're finding not only the television, the electricity and the insurance and the water rates, you're paying other things. (Group of unemployed people, London)

State pensions were judged inadequate and were seen to impose severe restrictions on people's lives:

> I know ones who don't smoke, who don't drink and who don't go to bingo and who are living on a basic pension and who are living in London and find it really really hard. A basic pension. (Community centre users group)

> Pensioners can get caught in the poverty trap: if they've got a small pension then it just takes them out of benefit, like housing benefit, council tax benefit. paying for that just brings them back down again, so all that pension that somebody worked for has disappeared. (Group of unemployed people, Yorkshire)

People discussed the pensioners' Christmas bonus:

> The thing is when we first got this ten pounds at Christmas many years ago it was worth ten pounds. Ten pounds now is not worth ten pounds.

> It's never been increased has it?

> Never been increased. I mean ten pounds is nothing is it? They should have increased it. (Community centre users group)

Women talked about the introduction of the Child Support Act and the ways it made things worse. It was perceived as another cause of poverty:

> The Child Support Act, that's trying to put single mothers below the poverty line. We're already struggling to make ends meet now and the Child Support Act are trying to reduce our benefits even more. (Group of women involved in campaigns)

Participants linked problems with low levels of benefit with the reduction of additional allowances:

> I think one of the big problems now or today is like social security, there's been a lot more stringent measures put on whereby when you're claiming you can't claim as much as you used to be able to do. Now some years ago when I was first unemployed I could claim for things like an allowance for washing and so forth, you can't do that now. So such as that used to give you an extra couple of pounds a week and I feel that nowadays such grants for buying clothes and so on, you could get them at one time and now you can't. (Group of disabled people)

The introduction of Social Fund loans to replace most grants was seen to make budgeting even more difficult:

> I might never be able to afford a three piece suite unless someone gave me one. Your carpets wear out. At one point you could go and get a grant from the DSS and that. That's gone by the by. They'll say to you, take a loan out. I can't afford to pay the loan back. I can't live on what they give me now and I'm not extravagant. I buy a book occasionally but there's not really a lot of money free for anything. (Group of lone parents, Yorkshire)

> In the situation of poverty, so many people are being denied the likes of grants, community care grants and stuff like that and when they originally came in they were supposed to be independent to help people in poverty, the expenses that they need help with … Now they can't apply for this extra help when they need it and when they need help they need it that day or the next day. It's not like seven days waiting for your knock-back from the DSS and being offered a loan which you're going in more debt for the next six months or a year. It doesn't make sense. (Anti-poverty youth group)

A member of a group of young people said that even grants were insufficient:

> You get a grant to move somewhere, you get money to buy things and then, that's it. You buy the things and then you're basically skint again. You can't afford the things you really want.

Another talked about the inadequacy of benefits for carers:

> And about caring for families. I lost my job, a few years ago, I'm talking. When you've got a father who actually was disabled, couldn't work, retired, and when it comes down to the one son to do everything on £54.00 a week. When you've got to help to wash them, shave them. dress them, take them to the toilet and things like that, and when a person's getting no thank you … other people get the fat of the land with bus passes and things and where carers, us carers, when we've got to take the person out who's disabled, and we carers we can't get anything. (Group of unemployed people, London)

The effects of not receiving your benefit on time were graphically illustrated by the personal experience of one mother:

> If I don't get my giro on time, they, like, pay nine days later. Some days you have to wait nine days for your giro and the hassle that you

get trying to get your giro. You have to borrow money to phone them up, or if you go into the office you have to sit down there for hours on end. A lot of people are down there with their children, they've had no sleep and these children are starving waiting for the giro and they don't care – you're just a number. And they expect you to keep self-respect. (Women's discussion group)

A homeless man commented on the social security system's inability to cope with high levels of unemployment:

I think one of the major problems is that the benefits system at least as originally envisaged by Beveridge ... was never designed to cope with the sort of unemployment levels which we have now. (Group of homeless people)

These comments from two lone parents, talking about voluntary work in relation to benefits, begs the question 'what is work?' and highlights the restrictions that volunteers face when claiming benefits:

I might go round and help my next-door neighbour ... Is that being a good neighbour or is that voluntary work? ... If every volunteer stopped doing stuff in this country, this country would run into a wall.

You go to the DSS to ask them for something and they say, 'I'm sorry, I don't know. This is something like going to do voluntary work. We'll have to go and check it out'. And they don't know and yet they're coming out with all these threats of workfare, which is voluntary work, and if they can't tell you whether looking after your neighbour is voluntary work, how are they going to enforce something like that? It's putting sharp divisions on people that are unemployed and people that are working. (Group of lone parents, Yorkshire)

The problem of trying to get a definitive answer from the DSS in response to enquiries about benefits, suggested by these comments, was spelled out in detail by this participant:

One of my major problems at the moment is to contact anyone in authority who is capable of changing what is obviously needed to change, your rights. You fail completely on dealing with the people whose job it is specifically to deal with individual things. Having failed that, you legitimately, you think, are entitled to go above them to those in authority who administer whatever the problem may be. You do so, you find usually you address things to them, they are bypassed. They never see it. Some time later they acknowledge it in retrospect and say it has already been passed, even admitting they've never seen the letter, passed to somewhere else and they're back to the people who caused the disturbance in the first place. It's chaotic, it's frustrating and you never get anything done even on the important things. (Group of older people)

BENEFITS AND 16-TO-18-YEAR-OLDS

Many participants thought that changes which had been made to benefits for 16-to-18-year-olds, which excluded them from payment, made young people extremely vulnerable to poverty. This had important implications for their families too. Their parents might have to keep them:

They're not given benefit until they're 18 years old.

It's a bad policy.

Well it's a bad policy but that creates poverty as well. It doesn't just create poverty, it creates disharmony in the family because if you've got a teenager who can't get a job and they've got no income coming in, you've got to keep them here. I mean once he becomes 16 your benefit has stopped altogether, if you're on social security, your benefit has stopped so you're actually keeping a 16-year-old so I mean that makes it even worse. (Group for low income families)

16-, 17-year-olds, they can't even buy clothes. They'll not be able to go out anywhere for a night out to the pictures, any money to go out with their friends. I think it could put them in a depression. It can lead them to feeling useless and hopeless and don't have anywhere to go. They've got to rely on their parents. If their parents are unemployed they're in an even worse state, so they are. It's just totally demoralising for them, it doesn't give them any hope. (Community centre users group)

These two participants also criticised youth training for not providing jobs at the end. A member of the same community group:

The 16-to-18-year-olds they leave school at 16, they're not entitled to unemployment benefit so they either have to take the YTS scheme or rely on their parents. And the YTS schemes, most of them don't pay more than £40 a week so then they have travel expenses and their lunch, they're not left with anything so they're suffering as well. Some of them are prepared to go out and work for that amount of money but they're not guaranteed anything at the end of it.

You look at the training schemes that they have around. They will put these children in schemes. Even from school, they don't mean them to do well. If they do well they're extraordinary. Then they put them in schemes that don't work. My son, two or three years ago, they took him into a scheme with a computer business. He was there for a whole year, after six months he was just going to this place, signing off, and then they could send him home again, because he was there for a year. After a year he could not get a job. Then a month after he was got rid of the people told him he should sign on to get another course. (Women's discussion group)

The transition from temporary work to claiming benefits was difficult for this young male:

Most young people, especially if they've got a record of being unemployed or any other reason why they might not have been working in the past, or anything like that, now they just have to do temporary work. So it lasts a couple of weeks, so then that screws their Income Support up. You know, is it worth me going out and getting a job because the length of time they have to wait between a job and getting the Income Support sorted out again. It's a bit frustrating isn't it? (Group of young people)

BENEFITS AND LOW PAID WORK

In recent times the political Right has argued that existing benefit levels act as a disincentive for claimants to look for work by encouraging 'dependency'. Participants in these discussions turn this notion on its head. They say that it is low paid work which means that people are forced into reliance on benefits because it leaves them worse off, even though benefit levels are inadequate:

Benefits start low ... If there's lots of jobs people can get, they are very low paid and people, I think, get to the stage that they think why work for 'x' amount of pounds when I can get 'x' amount of pounds from the dole. They're not any better. (Group for low income families)

You're worse off often in waged jobs, in low waged jobs, than you are on benefits because by the time you lose your benefits, free school meals, free prescription, right to housing benefit, even things like reduced prices into swimming and things ... and then you've paid your child care, it's much worse. (Group of women involved in campaigns)

There was a lot of agreement when one mother said:

When I was working I paid my childminder, I had to pay rent and then I had bus fares, I had to pay for the girl's dinners at school, I never got any grants that you got off the social security, so I lost out on all them. And when I became pregnant I went up to the Citizen's Advice to see about maternity benefits and they told me I was actually working for ten pounds less than what I would get on the social security, and I had been doing this for a year. it was my milk tokens, the girls' clothing grants for school, their free meals. (Group for low income families)

These issues were a particular concern for women:

You've got to earn so much to cover social security. Social gives so much and if you've got younger kids you've got to think about crËche, baby sitting and all that, pay full Council Tax, pay full rent and you've got to go for further education to learn to get one of those top jobs so you can earn all the money to cover all that.

... You've got to have a higher paid job, in this village you've got to have a job that at least will fetch ... for him to provide for me and for kids and all rent paid ... two hundred and fifty pounds a week and there's no jobs going for two hundred and fifty pounds, so what's the point if I'm taking out of social? (Members of a women's group)

A group of lone parents from Yorkshire said:

Both of my parents work but they're poor.

And the people that are working on a low wage are just as badly off as I am.

Well wages are bad. They're not getting the free prescriptions and things like we get ... they're probably no better off than that what we are, we haven't got any mortgage to pay and no council tax.

And they've got the fear of redundancy and stuff like that.

GENERAL SOCIAL POLICIES AND ISSUES

Some participants identified causes of poverty which were related to broader social policies and social issues. The two main ones which they talked about related to the lack of affordable housing and issues relating to structural discrimination.

HOUSING ISSUES

Five groups argued that the cost of housing when living on a low income caused poverty. Private landlords especially were criticised for raising rents above the levels of benefit and benefit increases:

> Private landlords ... Now they wrote me a letter last year asking for twenty pounds a week on my rent. The Government last year gave me a pound a week. I went to a tribunal and they're useless. They said, 'I'm sorry, you have a very good case, but there's little we can do' ... The Government says, 'Look, it's nothing to do with the Government it's between the landlord and you' ... Eleven pounds a week I had to pay. (Group of older people)

> Lack of decent housing. I mean you've got private landlords who are all over the top with the rent. Compared to London it's cheap, but 'round here they're atrocious, it's two hundred, three hundred pounds a month. People 'round here can't afford that. You only get allowed so much from the council, you have to put the rest yourself from the dole so they just can't afford to do that. Paying extra rent it means there's less snacks on the table for the family. It makes a bloody big difference not having a wage coming in. (Group of unemployed people, Yorkshire)

There was also a feeling that private landlords did not want claimants as tenants:

> There's a situation of fear from landlords – they don't want DSS. (Group of homeless people)

'Social housing' was viewed by this disabled person as perpetuating poverty by offering sub-standard accommodation which it is difficult to refuse:

> If you are down they tend to try and knock you further down. I mean, if you'd have seen the place that they gave my daughter and she couldn't turn it down, she couldn't say no, I'm not having that, like everyone else can. She's got to take it because that's the only thing

they're going to offer her because she's down and she's got nothing else. You never saw such a hole in your life. You wouldn't have wanted to live in it but she couldn't say no ... As far as they're concerned it's not their bloody fault so get on with it. 'We give you a roof over your head so like it or lump it'. (Group of disabled people)

STRUCTURAL DISCRIMINATION

Some participants saw structural discrimination as a prime cause of poverty. Provision of services for disabled people, for example, was described as negligible:

In the area that I stay in they're completely lacking in anything for disabled people in a position of poverty. It's unreal ... the service response to disabled people is – crap is a good word, that's being nice about it. (Anti-poverty youth group)

You almost feel that you're being punished twice. You're punished for being disabled, for not being allowed to work because places aren't accessible and they aren't flexible enough, and then you're punished for not working by being stuck on the benefit system which is totally inadequate. (Group of disabled people)

The same person commented on the discrimination which disabled people faced from government and employers:

It's also a fact that the Government say there's not enough registered disabled people to fulfil the quota. That's because people don't register, because you know damn well sometimes if you fill in an application form that says you are disabled, if you put a tick in there, you're not going to get an interview.

A disabled women spoke about the way finances were also a problem for disabled people:

Lack of money and resources is the main obstacle to people with disabilities being able to do the things we really want. It's what makes a physical disability into a social disability, a social disadvantage. (Group of women involved in campaigns)

Another participant talked more broadly about discrimination:

Ethnic minorities, disabled people, probably HIV as well, the homeless. There's an inter-relationship between disadvantage and poverty. It could be economic, it could be racial, sexual or physical, mental disadvantage. It gives you a much much higher risk of becoming a victim of poverty if you suffer from this disadvantage. (Group of homeless people)

SUMMARY

Participants' analyses of the causes of poverty can be divided into two main categories, related to individual and structural explanations of poverty:

INDIVIDUAL EXPLANATIONS

A small number of participants saw the causes of poverty in terms of individual agency.

STRUCTURAL EXPLANATIONS

The large majority of explanations put forward by participants related the causes of poverty to social structure, although they did not lose sight of their own agency in dealing with poverty. These explanations can be grouped into five broad categories. These are:

- Unemployment
- Politico-economic, which some saw as derived from the adverse effects of market economics, causing economic exploitation both in Britain and abroad
- General government policy, particularly in relation to privatisation and wage differentials
- Social security policy, particularly low benefit levels, new restrictions on benefits, particularly for young people and the inferior operation of the benefit system, coupled with availability of only low paid employment
- General social policies and issues, in particular housing and structural discrimination

5
The effects of poverty

In this chapter, people present their perceptions of the effects of living in poverty. They had much to say about the effects of being poor. It was much less a matter of trying to encourage them to speak, than making sure they were able to raise all the points they wanted to make. We asked people a range of questions, for example, 'What effects do you think being poor has on people?'; 'What do you think are the worst things about being poor?'; 'Does being poor make people different in any ways?'. Frequently, however, what actually happened was that people would move on to discuss such issues before we had come to ask the questions. This meant that they developed their own discussion and agenda, without our intervention.

We were at pains to make clear to people that we were not primarily concerned with the effects for them personally, because we wanted to avoid the conventional research focus on people's individual experiences of poverty and we did not want to be intrusive. Sometimes, nevertheless, people wanted to talk about personal experience, or to use it to illustrate more general points. People seemed comfortable talking about the personal, sometimes intimate issues which poverty raised for them, for example, the effects of poverty on relationships.

One question which was difficult for some of the groups was: 'What would it mean for someone not to be poor?' We had asked this question to try and offer people an alternative way of approaching the subject. But the question did not really bring out participants' own conceptualisations of poverty. Often they would answer as if the opposite to being poor was being rich and offer their own personal wish list, or alternatively, offer the positives to the negative effects of poverty which they had already identified. It is perhaps not surprising that people who are rarely, if ever, asked for their views and opinions about poverty, feel more comfortable talking about more tangible things, such as the consequences of poverty and its effects on them, something which they could feel they know about.

This reflects the experience of movements like the women's, black and disabled people's movements. To begin with, people seem to feel more confident and comfortable talking about what they are most familiar with. As they begin to take part in discussions and become more involved, they gain in confidence and skills and they feel increasingly able to explore broader issues.

The discussions we undertook made clear that people's views of the effects of poverty were overwhelmingly negative. The effects they identified fall into four broad categories:

- Psychological: highlighting psychological and emotional issues, such as loss of self-esteem, feelings of powerlessness, anger, anxiety, depression and boredom associated with poverty;
- Physical: exploring health issues relating to being poor;
- Relational: focusing on how relationships and social interactions are affected;
- Practical: including the practical implications of living in poverty for day-to-day choices, budgeting and child-rearing.

We now look in more detail at what participants said about each of these effects of poverty.

THE PSYCHOLOGICAL EFFECTS OF POVERTY

These took a number of forms which could affect different people and the same people at different times. Twelve of the 20 groups discussed the psychological pressures involved in living on low incomes. A member of the LETS group argued that these pressures are particularly acute for families living on low incomes:

> I think psychologically poverty can be a big pressure on people that are poor and that families that have children and have needs ... are really demanding.

POWERLESSNESS AND LOSS OF SELF-ESTEEM

One mother talked about the loss of dignity incurred by living on a low income:

> Poverty strips your dignity. You can't have any dignity with poverty. Where I come from you've people, like they go to the supermarket, they haven't got enough money to pay for what they need. And how does that person go home and say to the children that they haven't got enough food in to feed them? (Women's discussion group)

Another participant discussed the feelings of powerlessness which people who are poor experience:

> Poverty affects your self-esteem, your confidence things like that, basically. You feel totally powerless ... It has a major major impact because money is power basically. If you've got money, you've got the power to do what you want when you want. If you've not got that money, you've not got the spendability, you feel powerless because you can't do a lot of things, you can't live up to the expectations that people have. I'm kind of criticising myself, but I'd like these jumpers and all the fancy names and that. Folk have expectations and trying to live up to it and all that though you're powerless and you've got no money. (Anti-poverty youth group)

STRESS

Stress and constant worry were big factors for people:

> It causes fear. It causes humiliation, rejection, stress.

> Terrific stress. (Group of lone parents, Yorkshire)

> Constantly worrying, twenty-four hours a day about money and having to manage for the rest of the week, month, year, whatever. (Lone parent's group, Bristol)

Parents talked about stress becoming especially acute when festivals and holidays had to be budgeted for:

> I think also it's the stress that's overlooked – the actual stress that this causes. I think especially at the times when people are trying to do something for their children like birthdays and Christmas, you find you're just about managing on your budget, try to do something extra. Whatever you're on, you still want to provide for your children – well in our family you want to. (Rural tenants group)

This stress could also be transmitted to children from low income families:

> What really gets me is the way I feel about poverty. It's like kids saying we're going away to get a cheap holiday in a couple of weeks. The kids are saying, 'Can you afford it mum? Can you really afford it?' My kids get stressed about that ... It's not something that kids should have to be worried about, money, it really isn't.

> Of course it isn't, they should have a childhood and they don't have a childhood now. (Lone parent's group, Glasgow)

DEPRESSION, ANGER AND ANXIETY

About half the groups thought that living in poverty resulted in depression, for example:

> I think it causes depression and psychiatric problems because, my husband, he's got depression and I'm sure it's connected with being poor. (Group of unemployed people, London)

> It makes you more anxious and miserable. (Group of unemployed people, London)

> It's deterioration of the human spirit. (Group of older people)

> Sometimes I wake up and think, 'Oh, this is so boring'. It's the boredom of poverty and the boredom is what wears you down and makes you despondent in the end. I try to find jobs and I look around and then I think there's no point, they're not out there, the salaries are not out there, the child facilities are not out there ... It's deadly boring having to penny pinch all the time. (Member of LETS group)

One woman thought that depression resulted from the constant worry of trying to budget on a low income:

> Some might get depressed about thinking all day, sitting in the chair thinking all day, how am I going to pay the gas bill, the electricity bill, the water bill, the TV licence? How am I going to shop? Where's the next meal coming from? And it goes on. (Women's discussion group)

Again, budgeting for festivities was a source of depression:

> More depressed ... because you know you can't afford to buy anything. I mean Christmas and birthdays is when you dread most because you know you haven't got the money. (Group for low income families)

This depression was often exacerbated when children had to be cared and budgeted for too. Another woman talked about coping with children when she was a depressed lone parent:

> It's a multitude of things that are just going on in your head, churning over. J remember when my kids were little I couldn't sleep at night. I literally had a nervous breakdown when my children were little and I ended up in a psychiatric unit a few times ... I couldn't cope with it. (Women's discussion group)

Anger was commonplace :

> Anger, everything, your emotions just run riot. (Women's discussion group)

Another member of the same group said that not being able to give your children what they need, provokes a mixture of anger and depression:

> I get angry a lot. I get angry and I get depressed because my eldest is 12 and she's wanting these trainers that's £90 because someone else has go one and she can't have that. And I can't explain to her that she can't have them. (Women's discussion group)

Anger was also the result when ever harder restrictions were forced on families:

> It can make you very aggressive ... I really can't afford to have three bars on the fire because even though it's bloody freezing, so you say to the kids, right, put on another jumper or take a hot water bottle to bed. That angers me because why should you be cold? But because you are on a very low income and electricity is expensive, that's what you have to do. (Lone parent, Glasgow)

The sheer frustration of being not able to find work could prompt some people to take more desperate action, such as attempting suicide:

> I used to belong to the Job Club and this chap was really looking for work hard, really really looking for work. And he thought he had a job and he came in to celebrate then they told him the job wasn't his and he tried to kill himself because he'd looked so long. (Group of unemployed people, London)

Another unemployed person believed that the unsuccessful search for employment was a definite cause of depression:

First of all you go in full of enthusiasm thinking, yes! I was willing to do practically anything because I've worked in hospitals and domestic and school cleaning. I couldn't even find those jobs. And yes, you begin to get depressed and it does affect you. You do become a different person. (Group of unemployed people, London)

'HOW PEOPLE TAKE IT'

Another member of this group, however, thought that depression was not an inevitable consequence of poverty, but that it depended on an individual's ability to cope with the pressures of being poor:

You're talking about depression, I think this depression is because people let it get away with them. I don't suffer from depression, I've got worries, I don't let the depression get on to me. It's all about how people take it. (Group of unemployed people, London)

This discussion between unemployed people from Yorkshire about job-seeking, shows that negative psychological effects could also make people 'more determined':

You get fed up.

It makes you think differently.

It makes you harder, I think it makes you a lot harder ... more determined.

PHYSICAL EFFECTS OF POVERTY

One homeless person underlined the relationship between psychological and physical health:

It's not good for your health either emotionally or psychologically which can lead to physical problems just because the pure stress of trying to get by and pay the bills. (Group of homeless people)

Participants in eight groups commented that being poor had adverse physical effects on people. Many of these participants believed that poverty meant that good food had to be sacrificed because of lack of money:

The basic thing that we need is nutrition, good nutrition. (LETS group)

People thought that limited budgets forced poor people to eat cheaper, usually less healthy foods:

> And there's the stigma of the health. You want to get your child healthy food but you can't afford it. you want to go for the organic stuff but where is the money going to come from? (Group of women involved in campaigns)

> Worst thing about being poor, you can't go to the supermarkets and buy top quality food like they advertise on the telly and things like that. (Women's group)

> A lot of people go without food, definitely. I would say that the majority of young people that come in here don't eat properly. And when they do they just go for bags of chips and things like that, cheap things. (Young people's project)

One woman thought that if the diets of poor people were improved, it might have beneficial effects:

> Maybe if their diet was improved their life would be completely changed ... they'd have a bit more energy. (Women's group)

Another woman had more to say about tiredness. She related a personal story of the effort required just to go shopping when you are poor:

> You're more tired. I mean just the thing that being poor is so much work, your whole life. You see people going into a shop they buy what they want and they leave. But you're there, you're having to calculate how much money you've got as you go 'round, you're having to look at one brand then another, and meanwhile the store detective is looking over your shoulder which is also work having to cope with that kind of scrutiny, because you're poor they expect you to take something ... There's that pressure there all the time. (Group of women involved in campaigns)

RELATIONAL EFFECTS OF POVERTY

POVERTY AND RELATIONSHIPS

Half the groups who took part in the study thought that being poor had destructive effects on personal relationships between partners and within the family:

It breaks up marriages. (A member of a women's group)

A member of a disabled people's organisation illustrated the problem with an example of family breakdown which affected his daughter:

> My daughter and her husband and family had a good living and a nice home and her husband lost his business – it went to the wall – and they split up. The kids went haywire and one left home and the other one got pregnant ... My daughter, she lost everything, and I mean it, after twenty years of marriage. She's now living on £42.00 a week and she's really, really finding it hard and she just had nothing. (Group of disabled people)

Participants also thought that relationships with children suffered:

> It's also a kind of tension on your relationships as well because it really does spoil your relationships with people that you care about because you might not be able to give your kids what they want and so you're battling with them about their demands. (Group of women involved in campaigns)

Participants also talked about the introduction of particular policies which caused stress and conflict particularly affecting relationships between parents and children. For example:

> You must lose self-esteem because you're trying to cope with society and they ... brought in the Poll Tax, that was one of the most devastating things that anybody could do to a family. Because what it does, if you cannot pay and the children cannot pay, you turn the parents against the children ... you're turning against each other. (Group of women involved in campaigns)

Unemployed people talked about the ways becoming unemployed cut people off from social networks and relationships:

> I think if you've got a job with like a social circle and social contact, that's gone hasn't it? (Group of unemployed people, London)

For another participant the same was true of being homeless:

> Just to be able to go out and mix with people. It's not just having a social life in the first place, you don't meet people, you don't make contacts, you don't develop in any way ... it just restricts your opportunities. (Group of homeless people)

This woman saw isolation as a consequence of being poor. Isolation then further undermined relationships:

> The isolation ... that in itself means that you have more chances of your relationships not working because you're isolated. (Group of women involved in campaigns)

This participant thought that low income, debt, and relationships were inter-linked and the mounting stresses of living on low incomes had further negative consequences for relationships:

> You don't pay one of the bills and you get into debt and the whole stress of this cycle that builds up then has repercussions in your relationships with other people. (Group of homeless people)

POVERTY AND STIGMA

We did not ask people specifically about stigma. We deliberately did not use the word. But it was an issue to which they repeatedly turned. Almost every group discussed stigma as a key consequence of being poor. Stigma shaped, overshadowed and was the context for their relationships with other people, particularly their relationships with non-poor and official agencies.

> Poor is a stigma. (Group for low income families)

Attitudes towards poor people were thought to be extremely negative:

> It's other people's attitudes ... It's other people's attitudes. (Lone parent, Glasgow)

> ... just treat you like shit. (Young people's project)

> They look down on them as if they're beneath them. (Group of disabled people)

A personal illustration of how people on low incomes believe they are perceived as dishonest, was given by this member of a LETS group:

> I don't think people on low incomes are perceived to be honest. We gave up our television within two days of having the licence due because I thought that's it, we're not going to be able to afford this. I got rude reminders from some of the licensing people ... You're on benefits, you've got a television stashed away ... That is, I think, such a dreadful assumption.

A common view among participants was that poor people were seen as all the same and deviant:

They class you all together as a class, just because you're poor you commit crimes and stuff like that. (Women's group)

This unemployed woman described the effects of being lumped together as 'other' by a group of people with whom she was already well-acquainted:

Even in the church which belong I to, when they were collecting, somebody said,"We're collecting for 'you people'". I thought all of a sudden I have become 'you people', you know, whereas before, my husband, my ex-husband, and I were in all these groups and we were quite up on the upper thing and now I've become 'you people', that's how it affects you. (Group of unemployed people, London)

Unemployed people would be adversely stereotyped in all kinds of situations:

They make out unemployed people, they make out they're a step down from working class people, that's the way they make it out definitely. So if a working bloke has done something and he hasn't done it and they go to court with a suit on, then the solicitor will say, 'Yes, come on, he's working hard' and then they get off usually. If someone's unemployed they think, 'No'. And it's the working people that should be fined not the unemployed people because that's what makes them turn to crime. The Government don't know and they think, 'fucking hell'. (Group of young people)

Participants discussed the stigma that was felt by people claiming benefits at some length. Most participants, many of whom received benefits themselves, believed that non-claimants labelled claimants negatively, as 'scroungers' or 'lazy'. For example:

It's the way everybody reflects on you. I mean you're either a scrounger or a beggar or whatever. Well you're definitely a scrounger if you want a state benefit.

Is that one of the worst things about living on a low income, that people think you're a scrounger or lazy or ... ?

Aye, I mean there's a lot of people saying you don't want work.

Well that's not true, if I could work I would.

Exactly I was just going to say. I mean I've something wrong with me. I can't work but I'm still reflected as somebody who doesn't want work to some people's eyes – a scrounger. (Rural tenants group)

This lone parent felt embittered that she had worked in the past, paid tax and national insurance but was still made to feel like a 'scrounger' because she claimed benefits:

> A lot of single parents have actually worked and are paying their share. A lot of people seem to think we're scroungers who've never done anything in our lives ... we've all contributed to the Chancellor's pocket, we're only surviving on what we deserve to survive on and there is an attitude that the whole idea about scroungers and scrounging and getting what we're not supposed to be due, but we've paid for that, we've worked, we've paid out taxes. (Group of lone parents, Bristol)

This unemployed claimant from London believed that claiming benefit was definitely a stigma and provokes changes in attitude on the part of other people:

> I think you notice the way other people's attitudes towards you change once someone knows you're on invalidity benefit or the dole their attitude will blatantly change towards you. (Member of Group of unemployed people, London)

Claimants also commented on how they were treated by the benefits system. Some claimants said that they are made to feel as if they were not entitled to the benefits they received:

> It's a stigma that you actually feel you're grabbing something that you're not entitled to. You know, you've worked all your life to do something, I mean I found that. (Group of disabled people)

> When you go to the DSS to sign on you're treated like a criminal, as if you're going to cheat the country out of a fiver and stuff like that. It gets to the pitch where you think, well, everybody's working on the black economy? I wish I could join them. (Group of lone parents, Yorkshire)

Several groups expressed their concern about and dissatisfaction with the way in which claimants were treated by staff administering benefit payments:

> You've only got to walk in to any DSS office and watch how the staff treat the clients. They don't treat them like equal human beings, they treat them like dirt most of the time. (Group of disabled people)

> I mean I won't let other people know how poor I am ... I've been to

the social security and they make you feel exactly as if you're dirt. People who make you feel as if you're nothing. I've always worked, now I can't work. I can stand up for myself but there's thousands of people out there who can't stand up for themselves and are made to feel as if they're nothing. They're not even allowed to have the luxury to have a bit of pride in themselves because it's knocked out of them. (Lone parent's group, Glasgow)

... Establishment. It tends to be people in positions of power, like social security. They treat you like they own you, like it's coming out of their pockets a lot of the time. They begrudge you the little few pounds that you can get to scrape by. (Group of lone parents, Bristol)

The first time my husband was made redundant he went with his cheque to the post office, the man behind the counter literally threw his money through the thing ... I said, You don't do that to my husband ... That's how people treat you. (Group of disabled people)

Participants thought that the media had a central role in creating and perpetuating such negative images of claimants (see also Chapter 6):

The media campaigns during the middle or late 'Eighties, things about Costa Del Dole and benefit fraud and so on and so forth. They gave their readership the impression that everyone who's claiming is unworthy. Maybe they did it for political reasons or for circulation reasons but it's a pretty miserable intention. (Group of homeless people)

I was in the paper. I'd done something once and I was a student then so what it should have said in the paper was 'student smashing window' but instead it said 'unemployed man smashing window' which makes it look even worse. (Group of young people)

Some participants saw class and social stratification, as a cause of stigma. They thought that people near to the bottom of the system were viewed negatively by people further up it:

I think especially in this country because it's got a class system. It's more so here. Say you can be talking to people who call themselves 'upper class' or 'rich' or something, maybe get to know and talk to them. Once they realise you're out of work they just totally snub you altogether, cold shoulder, they just don't want to know you. (Group of unemployed people, London)

It's a class thing. I think you're seen again as being the lowest of the low, you know, morally. (A lone parent, Bristol)

According to this young person, people with jobs stigmatise unemployed people, seeing them as sub-working class:

> Working people look down on us definitely. I mean they're the working class in society, we're the non-working class. (Group of young people)

Members of this youth group thought that homeless people were especially vulnerable to the effects of stigma:

> You walk down that street you see it for yourself, people at the bottom end of the scale, the ones selling The Big Issue, folk stroll by with their nose in the air, just like that, it does my head in. The way they treat people in poverty. There's folk walking by ignoring them, don't give a damn about them.

> You see people sitting in the streets begging probably because they cannot find their way through the benefits maze and a normal office girl in her power-dressed mini-skirted suit and a fellow in his double-breasted pin-striped suit carrying his filo-fax and mobile phone, really look down their noses at them. (LETS group)

Some of the other participants singled out lone parents as victims of stigma. Lone parents themselves believed that they were a group who have been readily lumped together and labelled as deviant:

> Think of how the media portrays single parents.

> We've got a stigma that all our kids are going to grow up as child-murdering, glue sniffing, car joy riders and we're trying harder to make sure that they're disciplined, to get rid of that stigma. (Group of lone parents, Yorkshire)

Lone parents also spoke of the way that they were often compared adversely with the traditional nuclear family:

> I think single parents have a lot to prove because we're constantly being told that we're not a correct family; that we can't look after our children the same as a man or a woman in a relationship can look after children, a two parent family. It's almost like we're desperate to prove that you can look after your kids the same, more, or better than if you were a two parent family. I've never been into single parents' homes that were scruffy and I've met many single parents in poverty but they keep their houses nice, their kids really smart. (Lone parent's group, Bristol)

Some participants talked about the way physical appearance, particularly the clothes that people wear is a cause of stigma. They felt that poor people were often judged and then labelled on the basis of their appearance:

> I mean one of the things when I was at school; I remember wearing plastic shoes and it was a stigma and people were looking at you. I think this is one of the things about being in poverty, you feel that people are looking and saying he's not very good or whatever, I'm better than you. (Group of disabled people)

While the negative expectation of poor people is that they will be 'scruffy', as this participant said, if you don't conform to this stereotype and are on a low income, you can expect to be criticised too:

> If you're going out you're going to try and look dressed up. And I think then you get people's attitudes that they look and they expect you to be scruffy when you're unemployed. If you've got something new on they say, look at her, she must be working on the side or something, or somebody's buying this, that and the other for her. They don't think you can take care of your clothes or you've been in Oxfam or somewhere. (Group of lone parents, Yorkshire)

Members of two groups, however, sought a way out of negative labelling by trying hard not conform to the 'scruffy' negative stereotype:

> Because even I find myself telling children this – my grandmother used to tell us when we grew up poor, she used to say, 'You must not be poor and seen poor'. And I find myself telling the people around here, you mustn't be seen in poverty, you must try to do better. You must not be poor and seen poor. (Women's discussion group)

> I am poor and the whole family is poor but ... we try to make our appearance look good because if you don't you're being treated badly ... no-one wants to speak to you. (Group of women involved in campaigns)

Some participants talked about the stigma extending to where they lived, so that, for instance, credit was refused merely on the grounds that people lived in an area with a high proportion of poor people and a bad reputation:

> I suppose this is classed as a poor area and one of the effects it has on people is that people are on a low income and they don't get very much money so they can't even buy things. So you have to go for hire

purchase or credit. It's been proved in this area that you just have to mention that you're from this area and whether you work or you don't, it can stop you from getting hire purchase ... The thing is they don't have to give you a reason for not having credit, although they should, because they've got it all well taped. They can just say that you can't have it, they don't have to give a reason.

That's like if you go for a catalogue and you get the excuse, 'Well there's too many agents and we're not looking for any more agents, but thanks for the offer,' and you're like ...

They sent me an application form in the first place.

The thing is with that, with the catalogue, you get a refusal, the following day you get a letter from the same company saying we now require agents in the area, so if you could send in your first order again we will reconsider. And you still can't get it. (Group for low income families)

A member of the same group argued that, in her experience, it was not the fault of residents that areas became run-down and acquire negative labels. She thought that the reasons for change were complex and its effects upsetting:

It's not always had a stigma. I mean I'd say at one time ... this was a nice quiet area that people wanted to live in. I mean there's all different theories why but if you'd been here about five years ago ... it's completely changed.

PRACTICAL EFFECTS OF POVERTY

'DOING WITHOUT' AND BEING RESTRICTED

When we asked what they thought were the worst things about being poor, 17 of the 20 groups talked about the restrictions and the lack of choices it imposed. For this woman it meant doing without essential items:

The worst thing about poverty is doing without, not having the things that you want or need, you know, like not having the money for the food, not having the money to do things for your kids. I mean the worst thing is doing without. being on the poverty line you don't have the means, you don't have any choices. (Group of women involved in campaigns)

Young people talked about:

> Not being able to buy the new stuff you need, for the lifestyle, it's the cheaper stuff ... you've got to constantly budget and manage your money and try and stretch it out and think what you're going to do next week and how you're going to pay for it. (Anti-poverty youth group)

It can mean doing without branded food, as this lone parent explained:

> I go to the supermarket and buy own brand because that's what I can afford ... There's also going in shopping and not having enough money and having to put half the things back and these are essential things. You get to the cashier and have you got thirty pounds because it comes to thirty pounds? (Group of lone parents, Bristol)

It can mean doing without utilities:

> They're sitting in the dark. I mean I live in a complex where there are elderly people and they sit in the dark because they can't afford the electric. (Group of disabled people)

It can mean restrictions on your social life. Several participants said that budgeting for a social life while living on a low income was very difficult. Most followed a fortnightly boom and bust cycle from receiving a giro to having to manage for two weeks before receiving the next one:

> We are poor aren't we?

> You've only got one night a fortnight then you've got one day, of getting money so you can go out and feel good with money in your pocket.

> It's got to last two weeks you know.

> You're restricted, you're restricted. I used to go out every week, at least once every week.

> Live like a king for a weekend. (Group of young people)

> You don't go out very often do you, any of you? And if you do go out you suffer don't you for a couple of weeks because you've spent your money when you've gone out. (Young people's project)

> I mean I'd love to go out like once a week and go out and drink but sometimes I've got to rely on my friend to buy me a couple just to

keep me company. That's the only time I get to see her because she works during the week full-time but she'll see me at the weekend. (Group for low income families)

It curtails your social life definitely ... You can't go out when you want to, basically, and if you go out you're financially crippled for the next fortnight. (Group of homeless people)

Each fortnight we're waiting for the start of the fortnight to come so we can live it up a little bit and we keep that little bit of safety around us rather than venture out of it. And I'm as guilty as anybody that's what I'm saying. (Women's education project)

Sacrifices constantly have to be made:

The money we get is just liveable, isn't it? Just makes the ends meet the money you get.

Well, you just can't go daft. you can't go out every night.

I've stopped drinking and I don't smoke, so that helps a bit. (Community centre users group)

One woman compared the lives of poor people to those of prisoners:

I mean I'm not a single parent today but I have been a single parent, so I can speak from experience and I can also speak from experience from the people that live in my community. You know because it's rare they can afford to go the pub for a drink, they can afford to smoke – they're not prisoners for God's sake. You know, they think because a parent is on her own bringing up children, or somebody's unemployed and because they're unemployed they're not allowed to have any sort of life. (Women's discussion group)

Another member of the same group developed the theme:

People who are working, people who are fortunate enough to have a job, well they can afford to go out for a drink, well, they can afford to smoke, they can enjoy a social life. They're not prisoners, they've got a right to a social life. they've got a right to get away from the children maybe once a week. It seems like the poor are punished all the time. And I don't want to go into this too much but you'll get a prisoner, right, who's inside, deprived of everything. They've been deprived of their freedom, but they're not deprived of anything else. I mean I know a prison where it's stated categorically in the press where they get special money. I'm sure that a lone parent family or anyone who's

unemployed doesn't have any other money once they've bought food
... they're penalised all the time are the poor.

Poverty can affect people's access to leisure. A participant from a rural
tenants group in conversation with the project worker, said:

> It stops you doing a lot of things if you haven't got enough money.

> *What sort of things?*

> Like going on holiday. I mean half the time you can't even afford to
> get a carpet

It can also affect the way in which people use their leisure, for example,
the choice of soft drug-use over alcohol:

> People are more prone to drugs and getting off their head because it's
> a nice escape for a few hours.

> *Do drugs tend to be cheaper than drink?*

> Well it lasts a bit longer, do you know what I mean, the feeling.
> (Group of young people)

Lack of money prompted worries about funeral expenses:

> I wonder do they take it into consideration if I'll be dead tomorrow
> who will be paying for my funeral if the average funeral is two to three
> thousand pounds. (Group of older people)

People talked about their lack of access to transport:

> You're restricted to where you can go. Even to travel in the buses in
> and out of town, it's almost two pounds just to go in and out, and that's
> just one person. it's terrible for families. (Community centre users group)

They spoke again about the problems of buying clothes and maintaining
their appearance:

> You can't go out, like, and buy a nice pair of jeans – that would be
> half your giro. And all the lads are saying come on, come out. You've
> just got to go out and rob if you want to wear something decent.
> (Group of young people)

> I found that when I was on basic unemployment I couldn't cope if my
> shoes got holes in them. It was a problem if I needed new underwear –
> just simple things, it was a problem. Just to buy a bit of underwear is a
> problem and having your hair cut. Just having your hair cut is a

problem. (Group of unemployed people, London)

Options become more limited when special occasions have to be budgeted for as this exchange between two lone parents highlights:

> You're all right if there's no birthdays, it's not Christmas and you don't want to go on holiday and you haven't got a car and you don't smoke. if you're a good budgeter you find you can live on it, but when things come up ...

> But there's always something crops up that you don't expect and it's, Oh, _____ hell, where am I going to get the money for this. Because you can't borrow, you can't get a loan – well, if you can you're going to pay treble what it's worth. Nine out of ten you've lost your credit rating because of things that happened in the beginning when you were first out of work. (Group of lone parents, Yorkshire)

To make ends meet, choices have to be made which can then make things worse:

> Well you actually miss something else, say, like for example, if you buy like electric stamps, gas stamps or whatever, you'll say I'll miss that this week, we'll buy shoes, then say that the next week, the next week and then before you know where you are the bill's there and you just haven't got enough for the bill so you start missing something else to pay for the bills – it's a vicious circle. (Rural tenants group)

Some participants discussed the wider significance of the restricted choices in their everyday lives:

> It means we don't have choices. We don't have the option to do what we want to do. We're very limited both in what you actually do and when you do it. If you don't have money you can't get anywhere, so I mean that can be down to things like it's difficult to choose where your children can go to school. You don't have options like people who have more money, or like getting out of the area.

> It's a wider thing I think that whole thing about options, it's about having choices in life ... not being able to choose where you live, how you dress, what you eat even. Most of us would choose to eat better but can't afford it. Like you said, where your children go, education, and if you haven't got those choices it limits your power around what you can actually do about it. (Group of lone parents, Bristol)

> It's like being left out on life's basic choices, being able to choose what

school you want your kids to go to. You're restricted by how much you can afford to get them to school that's nearest whether it's good or not, and healthcare, everything – it all comes down to money in the end. I mean I get maintenance and so I get my healthcare paid for, but I can't afford to go to the dentist and I've got a rotten tooth in my mouth. That is something that is very basic I think, and that is something I can't have. Simple things for my children to go to clubs and things, everything. You're forced in to this domestic role where you're constantly counting pennies for really trivial things, but your life becomes very stuck in that, it becomes so restricted and the way you see life then also becomes very restricted and that's when I think problems do occur, outside your family as well as inside. (Women's discussion group)

RAISING CHILDREN ON LOW INCOMES

Many participants thought that the lack of choice imposed by poverty impacted most on parenting and children. Participants who were parents, especially lone parents, expressed their view that financial constraints meant that their children had to make sacrifices:

When you're not working and you're having to claim, you can't take your kids out to the shop and say can I buy you this? Can I buy you that? You can't. You've got to say, 'Oh, I'll try and buy it for you next time.' (Group of unemployed people, Yorkshire)

You imagine what it's like for a child in a poor family to see others with wealth and the wealthy children getting presents and the child come up to the parents of the poor family saying, 'Mum, dad, why can't I have this?' (Group of unemployed people, London)

I'm a lot stricter with my kid because all his mates from school go, 'Come on we're all off to the garage to buy ice-cream,' and stuff like this, and I say, 'Oh, no, not tonight, I can't afford it, no sweets'. Another kid would play up and his mum would say, 'Oh all right then,' because she can afford to give in. I'm a lot tougher that what his mates' parents are because they can afford to just let them have it and I can't ... They all go out getting invited to these parties and I think, Oh, God, that's another three quid just to get into this party or trips at school, things like that. I'm trying to keep him the same as the other kids who've got working parents and I'm finding it trouble. (Group of lone parents, Yorkshire)

As parents are expected to take more financial responsibility the situation gets worse. One woman saw the rising costs of education as a source of potential problems between parents and children:

> The schools are so financially demanding on parents and also they make parents feel guilty, you know, with these uniforms and day trips, holidays. You'll get some children who are better off in schools so they can afford to go on these holidays but the kids who come from lone parents can't go anywhere. How do these kids feel and how does the mother feel? (Women's discussion group)

Another said:

> I once had a letter from school, it was our Paul I think, and 'you've got to go and sort his shoes out'. I wrote, 'Dear Sir, I have got four children and it's not Paul's turn to have shoes, it's one of other lasses.' It took about three months before I could afford another pair of shoes. (Group of unemployed people, Yorkshire)

Several groups discussed the difficulty of affording designer trainers:

> They go to school and someone's got Nike trainers on and you've bought them a cheaper brand, they're not going to be pleased. (Women's group)

> You can actually sit with your money and if you go through it with your older children, that's what you're paying out on bills and food every week, and for a few seconds they can understand it, why you don't have the money, but they really don't understand because they're still going out on the street and their friends have got Reebok boots, or what have you, and they don't understand. They know where your money's going and they know you've got very little but they don't understand why other people's children can have these things. Like one of mine was using a felt-tip pen on his shoes because he was writing Reebok on them, a pair of cheap trainers. He thought I can rub that off and write Reebok ... You can accept it for yourself, it doesn't matter if you haven't got a pair of knickers without holes in or no stockings because you can cover up, that doesn't matter because you can accept it more for yourself, you can't accept it for your children and that's the worst thing. (A lone parent, Glasgow)

Participants highlighted the problems of buying new clothes for their children:

> I like to buy for my kids but I can't buy them what I want to.

I mean you need some new clothes but you think the kids need it more than I do.

So we make do with clothes for four or five years, or second-hand clothes. The kids, especially at school, you've got to spend. (Group of unemployed people, Yorkshire)

I save what money I've got to sort the kid's stuff out, I try my best. (Women's group)

A group of young people singled out the problems facing lone parents:

The mother who's a single parent can't afford to feed the wee ones. She does her best but with a lack of budget there she can only do what she can do. With the poor conditions she can't do anything about herself, hasn't anyone to talk to and doesn't even know how to go about taking action to get her living conditions seen. That has been a direct result of poverty because she's had to put so much time into her own life and organising things about the situation of poverty that she's in – looking after the house and stuff like that, that's at the back of her mind. (Anti-poverty youth group)

A PROBLEM OF 'DEPENDENCY'?

The idea of 'dependency' and assumptions about people becoming 'dependent' on welfare benefits, have become central to political and public debates about poverty. Many of the people who took part in the project were aware of the heated discussions there have been about 'dependency'. Most emphasised that they did not want to be dependent on benefits. Earlier in this chapter, we reported how stigmatising they felt the benefits system was. The consensus among participants seemed to be that reliance on welfare benefits was forced on claimants. They did not want to rely on them and, in most cases, they considered that benefits were inadequate and life on them harsh.

How can you want to live on benefits? If you analyse what people really get on benefits you can't buy nothing much. You can't buy proper shoes, you can't buy these fancy things that children would like, so why would you really want to live on benefits if that's the only thing? And you're having to go down to the DSS and talk to these people and people looking down on you. I assure you nobody in their right sense would want to be on those benefits, it's degrading. (Women's discussion group)

You can't totally rely on the state. People who are on income support or benefits of some kind cannot totally rely on the state because you don't have enough to live on. (Community centre users group)

Some people talked about being forced to depend financially on their families because of the inadequacy of benefits:

I think that a lot of families that are on benefit do rely on their families sometimes – they've got to. But I mean you maybe find in this area that the whole family's on benefit ... they can't basically help each other, families can't help each other.

I'm not so bad because if I run out of money for electricity or that, I can go to my brother or mum so it's a bit easier for me.

But not everybody's got that.

You don't like doing it either because you do feel like you're having to rely on them and I don't think it's fair on them because they've worked hard for that and you're having to borrow off them and then you're still skint by the end of the week anyway because you're having to give them it back. (Group for low income families)

I'm reliant on my mum.

I think it is true. My husband was unemployed with three small children at the time and we were relying on my parents as well ... if it wasn't for them then I wouldn't have been able to manage. (Members of a community centre users group)

A number of participants introduced another meaning to dependency, one which is less often discussed. They thought that being dependent upon benefits made it possible for the DSS to govern your life. For example:

You're also social security dependent and I think that's one thing that really pisses people off is relying on the social security and them being your god. They determine when you get paid, what you get paid, if you're going to get paid. They can muck you about and hold your book back for days ... so many people's lives are governed by the DSS. (Anti-poverty youth group)

As soon as you're on income support everybody officially knows your business ... you have to itemise every single thing. I had to do it weekly with receipts so I bought a pair of socks, this is how much they cost. I bought a mixer, this is how much it cost. And then I had permission to spend the money that I'd got to go on holiday … when we went on income support about two years ago we had three thousand pounds in the bank and they rang up to ask how much we'd got left of it, about what, three, four months ago. (Women's education project)

TRAPPED IN POVERTY

Some participants saw poverty as a trap, from which it was extremely difficult to escape once you were caught. According to this woman, povertywas a psychological and physical trap:

> Poverty is here. It's on our streets, it's in our cities. You can see it when you go outside, there's people begging. It's in communities, it is here in Britain and the government should start listening because there's people living in poverty, living with masses of problems. All these problems rub off on every member of the household, who, in turn, take out their problems on their children and it's a roundabout and you can't get off. Poverty drags people down mentally and physically and it's very hard to get out of the poverty trap. (Women's discussion group)

People's appearance suffers, making it more difficult to get employment:

> It's a catch-22 thing, once you get into that position … You can't afford to buy clothes so you haven't the clothes to go to an interview to try and get yourself out of it and you're accused of not trying. (Group of homeless people)

Trying to get a job when you come from an area which is stigmatised can also be difficult:

> It's like with the council. If you're unemployed and you go for a council flat they'll shove you in a shit area, right? And then when you go for a job interview they say, 'Where are you from?' And you tell them where you're from and they think, 'Oh, _____, we won't have him.' It's because this one's from this estate. So it's just a vicious circle. (Group of young people)

Budgeting on a low income is another trap:

> It's like you're going on a vicious circle here. You take out a loan about November to buy Christmas presents and you're still paying it off away until next October and then you've got to start again because you've never had a chance to be able to clear up and get on your feet

... It's a rob-Peter-to-pay-Paul situation all the time especially, say, if you've got a very bad winter and you're using your electricity and heating all the time. (Group for low income families)

Every year there's something else. This year it's the television that went and it won't be back. And next year I'll have to find something else. You keep getting rid. You're looking round in this big circle. (Lone parent, Glasgow)

Being on benefits leaves little room for manoeuvre. For example:

I went and asked at the hospital, 'Could I have a power wheelchair?' She says, 'Well, do you get mobility allowance?' I said, 'Yes'. She said, 'Well get one on that'. So I turned 'round and said, 'Well, how do I get and go places when I've given all my money to you?' So it's Catch-22. You just cannot do it because they won't let you. (Group of disabled people)

POVERTY AND CRIME

About half the discussion groups thought that there was a link between poverty and crime. Participants thought that the restricted choices that people face on low incomes forced them into crime:

Well there is crime where I live – actually it's subsided now, I don't know whether it's gone further afield but there is a lot of poverty and there's crime. How you tackle it I don't know because if people haven't got enough money to live on, what else can they do? They just get to the end of their tether and then they think, 'Well, what have I got to lose by taking something that belongs to somebody else?' What have I got to lose? Nothing. A bit of freedom for what, a few months locked up inside and let out again and start again? ... But the poor are punished, they're punished even before they turn to crime. The poor are punished because if they can't afford their electricity, their gas , their water, their television licence, they're taken to court and treated like criminals ... So they think, well, what have I got to lose? I'm going to be punished for not paying my bills so I might as well be punished for breaking in someone's house, or doing a bit of shoplifting. (Women's discussion group)

It _____ gets people into crime doesn't it? People _____ go out robbing and I like robbing because it makes me feel good because _____ I'm ripping someone else off that can afford to be ripped off, making some money out of it. But it's all just stupid, it's all just

_____ life isn't it? It ain't going to change. (An ex-offender and member of the group of young people)

This guy came out of the post office and he'd a wad of money in his hand and he stood there counting it. Now me and my mate had been out of work for about six or seven years at that time and we just looked at each other and the same thought must have gone through our minds. Do we nick it? It was something that we could never have done but we looked at each other and said this guy was easy, quick, down the back alleys and away. (Group of disabled people)

Now I mean when you're young, you think of all the ways of surviving. Crime is the first thing you think of. So a young mother turns to crime, just petty shop-lifting, they don't feel they're hurting anybody, they're not sitting at home being depressed about their problem. They feel that they're going out and doing somethingabout their problem. What society tells them is right and wrong – they lose all sense of that. You lose all sense of right and wrong when you've got children to look after. (A lone parent from the women's discussion group)

There are so many single parents that are living well below the poverty line. You hear this on the 'bread-line' for single parents; the bread-line is a luxury, I'm telling you. Because they're having to budget and everything that they get, you need the best for the wee one, and they forget about themselves. It's that vicious circle that they're in as well, having to steal because that's what it comes down to these days. (Lone parent, Glasgow)

Young people were seen as another group at particular risk of being forced into crime:

And what's worse now is that there's kids leaving school that are going to live on nothing all their life and they've got no expectations and then you're tut-tutting because they're stealing cars and doing this, that and the other. (Group of lone parents, Yorkshire)

This woman thought that fining offenders on low incomes only perpetuated poverty:

It annoys me when these people, who don't know what it is to be without their breakfast, sit on the bench, sitting in judgement of people who are living below the poverty line. They don't have a clue how they're living and they're dishing this out, putting fines, fines,

fines on people who can't afford to pay, so they're only driving more out to crime. I've got to pay this fine so I'll have to go and do this, do that, to pay the price. They're just encouraging crime all the time and I think if there was a fairer system it would save a lot of the government's resources like putting people in prison and all the other things they're trying to do to stop crime and they'll never stop it while there's so much poverty about. They'll never eradicate crime. (Women's discussion group)

You just can't get a car unless you just went illegal, then you get arrested and get into trouble, get fined and then it's taken out of your benefit so your benefit goes down. (Group of young people)

ACCENTUATING THE POSITIVE

Nineteen of the 20 groups highlighted the damaging personal and social effects of poverty but a small minority of participants also pointed to a more positive side to being poor, while not denying its damaging effects. They believed that despite the numerous restrictions placed on them by poverty, that there could also be some positive experiences:

On the up side you can make a lot more of your life, if you're looking at it positively and you see what's there for nothing. You've actually got time to do things that you couldn't do if you were working. You can concentrate on doing things for yourself, but you've got to be fairly strong-minded about it which is quite hard when you are struggling with the stress. (Group of lone parents, Yorkshire)

My sister said that ... when they were very poor she made a pound of mince last four days ... It is a challenge if you approach it in the right way ... it can be fun, it can be a challenge as long as you don't get beaten back. (LETS group)

It makes you more determined to get there. I mean I've been to college and how I get there – I mean the journey in a car is a journey but to have to do it on a bus with two kids is impossible. It's the fact that I actually get there is an achievement. (A lone parent, Bristol)

This member of an anti-poverty youth group thought that there could be positive psychological consequences:

This might sound daft, but it makes you a better person. It makes you stronger inside because you've got a lot more problems if you're in poverty than you would normally have if you were working. I know it seems a daft thing but if you're on an adequate income you've got less problems, you've got less worries. There's so many problems in between.

Community solidarity was still a positive consequence of the miners' strike:

> Places like this community pull together ever since the miner's strike. I mean I've never known a community like this one, everybody clubbed together. If anybody got ten pounds a week extra it got put in pot, everybody cooking food. If you walked in a pub to do a collection someone would say I'll get you a pint while you're in. Everybody pulled together. (Group of unemployed people, Yorkshire)

Some politicians have suggested that poor people lack the initiative and budgetary skills to cope on limited incomes (see also Chapter 6). Several participants in the project refuted these comments and stressed the creativity that poor people have to possess in order to manage:

> I think we've got to recognise the fact that it takes more brains to live on a few coppers on a low, low income than it ever does for these people that have got big salaries. (Group of older people)

> It takes a lot more skill to live on a low budget than it does for somebody who's maybe earning £500 a week. I mean compare £500 to keep a family of three or four, or whatever, and a family which I'm in with myself and three big children and just over a hundred pounds compared with, like, somebody with £300 maybe £500 a week. It speaks for itself, doesn't it? (Rural tenants group)

> We are the best economists in the country. We can budget on next to nothing. We're brilliant with money.

> And we're bloody good at dyeing and remaking things.

> We are the best economists. We are careful people. (Group of lone parents, Yorkshire)

SUMMARY

Almost all participants thought that the effects of poverty were overwhelmingly negative. The effects they identified can be grouped into four broad categories.

- Psychological effects: poverty was associated with loss of self esteem, feelings of powerlessness, anger, depression, anxiety and boredom
- Physical effects: poverty was damaging to people's health
- Relational effects: poverty adversely affected people's social and personal relationships and the stigma associated with it overshadowed these relationships
- Practical effects: poverty restricted people's choices and also made it difficult to bring up children

Stigma was identified as a key consequence of poverty. Participants felt stigmatised by other people's attitudes, the media, the benefits system and by where they lived. Some groups, like lone parents and unemployed people, were seen to face particular stigma.

Participants rejected the idea of 'dependency', emphasising that poor people want to live independently and not rely on benefits, but were instead often trapped in poverty. They thought that poverty pushed people into crime.

A small minority of participants also mentioned positive aspects of living on a low income, emphasising people's skills in budgeting, meeting the challenge of being poor and the community solidarity that can result from living in an area with a majority of people on low incomes.

6 Images of poverty

This chapter offers poor people's analysis of the images and language of poverty reflected in current media and political representations. We wanted people with experience of poverty to have a chance to offer their views and ideas about some of the key issues which have been identified in current public debates about poverty in Britain.

We wanted to do this in a way which would be as interesting and accessible as possible for participants. We decided to use newspaper stories which reflected these high profile issues. We selected four stories: two by journalists, one reporting part of a key speech by the then Secretary for Social Security and the last one headlining the 'underclass', an issue which has been central in both political and media debates about poverty. We chose them for being typical of the dominant poverty debate, while appreciating that there is no such thing as a representative news item.

While these issues relate to the previous government, particularly the speech by Peter Lilley, the issues which they address continue to be current. Concerns about the 'underclass', 'dependency', single mothers, begging and street living, are still central in both media and political discussions about poverty.

To ensure that everyone could take part in the discussion, we passed photocopies of the articles around in turn so that everyone could see them and tried to give people time to digest them. We also enlarged them to A3 size and held them up. To make sure that non-readers and people with visual impairments were fully included we also read them out.

This part of the discussions drew a particularly strong response from participants, although some did find it difficult. Almost all the participants seemed to read the cuttings with interest and answered spontaneously; they raised strong feelings. The predominant emotions expressed by participants were frustration and anger – tinged with sadness – at what was being said about them. Most seemed familiar with such stories and nobody showed any sign of disbelief at what they were reading. A few gave resigned shrugs. It was also a lively and active part of the project, with much moving about and exchanging of cuttings. While the tape recorder picked up people's comments, laughter and shouts, it could not do justice to their body language with much nodding and non-verbal agreement when participants challenged media poverty imagery.

The cuttings focus on 'welfare mothers', 'professional' begging, 'welfare queue jumping', especially by young lone mothers, and the 'underclass'. Participants give their views on each in turn; a final short section offers their more general thoughts about the media and poverty. There is more about their views on politicians and the government in the next chapter.

Heroic lessons in thrift for todays mothers

by Val Hennessy

READ THIS BOOK and you realise how lacking in initiative the 'working class' has become. Reeve's families didn't sit around feeling sorry for themselves and insisting that society should bail them out. Instead they made tremendous efforts to budget and be self-sufficient. I shall think of this book next time I'm stuck in the Tesco checkout queue. Have you noticed the sort of food todays 'low income' mothers pile into their trolleys?

Daily Mail 15 January 1994

STIGMA AND PEOPLE ON LOW INCOMES

This article provoked a lot of anger among participants. Many, like this woman from a group of disabled people, asked how Val Hennessy knew that the women in the article were 'low income mothers':

> So when she's studying this queue at Tesco presumably the low-income mothers have a big sign across their foreheads saying 'I am a low-income mother'.

This was echoed by this exchange between three lone parents. They argued that they didn't want to be reliant on state benefits, but that this was forced on them:

> How does she recognise low-income mothers in a supermarket, because they don't have tattoos on.

> I was just going to say, do they have a big sign saying, 'I'm a low-income mother' or something? But Yvonne, she worked so she wasn't on benefits but she was worse off ... and it's like you don't get enough with the benefits you're on, you'd like to work. I mean I think I could work but I'd be worse off than I am now.

> We don't want to rely on state handouts, we don't think we have a God-given ... I mean, I think we have a right to them because we paid taxes – you know, when we were working – but we don't actually want to stay on them. (Group of lone parents, Bristol)

Many people questioned Hennessy's need to judge and stereotype:

> Well she would then have something tattooed across her forehead: middle class pratt. (Group of homeless people)

Many participants saw this article as part of a wider campaign by government and the media, especially the press, to lay blame for all of society's ills on poor people:

> I think it's to throw single parents in a bad light or people on low incomes in a bad light, you know, to portray us as scroungers.

> It's oppression, it's just to hold us down. It's just like establishment, it's like we had an uprising and every single person who's living in poverty or every low income family got together and started really creating they'd be frightened and they just hold us down, sort of thing, with their opinions and other people. (Group of lone parents, Bristol)

> It's about keeping you under control ... that's really to stop you claiming.

> They are trying to blame us and not the Government. We're in this predicament because they say it is our fault when really it's down to the Government. (Group of women involved in campaigns)

There was agreement that the article was an attempt to jump on the anti-poor bandwagon:

> It's politically fashionable, with all this carry-on with young mothers and relying on the state and the Child Support Agency crap. It's

politically fashionable to write about this, but coming out with poxy statements like this: 'Reeves' families sit around feeling sorry for themselves and insisting that society should bail them out.' What the fuck's this statement. Effectively this is a good example of what I've said, the idea they shouldn't be relying on the state, they should be out working. (Anti-poverty youth group)

An unemployed woman made the point that moral judgements are always made against people who are powerless to resist them:

If you go back you discover that social workers at the time, they would go into a family; because the social workers were middle class, they would differentiate between the deserving and undeserving poor and they would look whether somebody had swept up, you know. And then they'd look 'round the house and they'd say well, we'll give you some money but first of all you've got to sell that and sell that. So they were forcing that because they had to sell things. And eventually, when they were really down, providing they were clean living, wholesome human beings and deserving of this charity, then they might get something; but it was very, very destructive of self respect. And that's the idea that people have now. State handouts, this dependency culture, well, it's a way of actually getting unemployed people and blaming the victim for the crime, you know. That's what it's all about. And fair enough, dependency culture ... What about the Civil List? Should we cast Charlie and Diana as being part of the dependency culture? They were on the Civil List. (Group of unemployed people, Yorkshire)

POVERTY AND INITIATIVE

A large majority of participants objected to the assertion that, today, people on low incomes lack initiative:

I don't like the 'lacking in initiative' of the working class, nonsense that is. (Group of older people)

As women do you think that you lack initiative when you get your money at the beginning of the fortnight, or week, or however you get it, working or not. Do you think that you can then say that the way you plan to run a house shows lack of initiative? Do you think that it's so easy to live on your money that really you don't need to work things out at all? (Rural tenants group)

Others took the implied lack of initiative to mean that living on a low income was characterised by fatalistic passivity:

> But that is suggesting that they all sit around feeling sorry for themselves. That stands out. It presumes that all people on low incomes and benefits are going to sit there feeling sorry for themselves.

> It seems like you can't do nothing for yourself if you're poor. Sit around and do nothing, that's what it seems, sit around and do nothing. (Rural tenants group)

Two women questioned Hennessy's ability to say that people on low income lacked initiative if she herself had no direct knowledge of it:

> She's never been in that position, I don't see how she's got the right to condemn.

> She won't know what it's like until she's tried it first hand herself. (Group of lone parents, Glasgow)

Some participants questioned how poor people could be lacking in initiative when many were forced to feed families, without even being able to afford to shop in supermarkets. Participants were not only forced to juggle with their finances, but they also had to use a number of shops in order to secure the food which was best value for money:

> I can't afford to go to Tescos! (Group for low income families)

Paradoxically, trying to save money by going to the cheaper stores could cause stigma as well:

> Ah, but she's on about being poor and about Tescos, you know Netto? If kids around here know you shop at Netto they will not eat or they will not walk 'round with you if you have a Netto bag.

> My mum won't go about with a Netto bag. (Women's group)

BUDGETING ON A LOW INCOME

Many discussions picked up the point of trying to eat healthily on a limited budget. People said that healthy food was much more expensive:

> They're buying cheap, unhealthy food because they can't afford to buy proper foods for their families – it's too expensive. (Community centre users group)

> I mean you compare a supermarket to a health shop and you could do your supermarket shop twice, three times, four times over to what you

could in the health shop. (Group of women involved in campaigns)

Most people taking part were extremely angry with Hennessey's suggestion that people could provide healthy diets by juggling meagre budgets:

> Well spit on you Val Hennessy! I'm thrifty, I can make a piece of meat last well. I know we eat it, but at the same time, I have £45, £50 to budget a week and when I cook food for my kids; they eat pretty well, they eat vegetables and fruit, but I'm not going to buy organic bread and stuff, although I'll eat it, because they will not eat it and the alternative is it gets thrown away. (LETS group)

Many people, like these two women, thought that changes in technology and economics made many of the skills advocated by Hennessy impractical today:

> I mean the point is that the fuel cost, the electricity and gas charges are so high that people can't afford to put their ovens on to do stew and dumplings.

> Turn of the century they had coal fires that heated the house, you cooked your food on it. Now they're separate. (Women's education project)

Buying in bulk in order to make food cheaper is almost impossible on a restricted budget:

> It's like buying those tiny little cans because you can't afford the bigger ones.

> Yes, which costs you more in the long. You can't buy big things of washing powder, you have to buy the 2lbs boxes every week that don't last two minutes. So we pay more out of the shopping in the long run.

> There's lots of things like that, and if you're like me and there's just the two of you, it's not worth buying a big tin because you just get fed up with it.

> Oh, I know, it's bloody awful.

> And you get fed up of having beans on toast. (Group of lone parents, Yorkshire)

Some queried the motives behind the assertion that low income mothers had their trolleys piled up with food:

You want to feed your child as best as you can, the best foods, and I don't think it's fair that we should condemn somebody for doing that. But what would she rather we did, feed them hamburgers and chips which we couldn't afford to do anyway? (Group for low income families)

The large majority of participants saw the low level of benefits as being at the heart of the problem. For example:

There's one significant lesson that the Government needs to learn, which is: when you find out what income support you've been awarded, and it splits it up and tells you whether this much for you, there's this much for your spouse, there's this much for your kids – their idea of what it costs to run a child is utterly without reality. They view what it costs to run a child as less that what it costs to run an adult. It's nonsense! (LETS Group)

Many thought that money should be made available to ensure that people eat healthy diets. Basics like cookers should be provided as a necessity:

My grand-daughter is 7 and my daughter has only just acquired a cooker because social security have said that they won't give her the money. Council houses no longer provide cookers, so how does she cook? (Women's education project)

Many participants thought that the situation now, even with the welfare state, was worse than in the 1920s and 30s:

I mean what was the quality of life like living on a penny a week and what's the quality of life just now? It's not improved any and it's getting worse, it really is, I have to say that. Attitudes like that – I can be totally sympathetic with the characters in that book, but I can't listen to somebody who's saying that people nowadays should go back to that and learn by that family's escapades in there. I really can't see that. What's happening now is we've gone back to Victorian times and it's the people, the young people who are suffering. Young single parents, young families who have come from families who have never worked, who have got nothing to look forward to, absolutely no future whatsoever. They don't want to rely on state benefits, they don't want to do that – they don't have a choice in the matter, they have to do it. (Community centre users group)

One group of participants, however, were bitter at the high rates of benefit which they thought that single mothers were receiving:

All I know, I can tell you, I've got one above me, a young lady of twenty-eight that's not married and the father's gone. They get more money than I do from the government and it makes me wild to think I fought for this country five years overseas. I never saw my wife for five years and I'm getting £60 a week and they get more than I do. They get free milk, no council tax. (Group of older people)

Some agreed with the argument that traditional budgeting skills were lost to this generation:

I think in a way some mothers who have got low incomes don't really know how to budget. I think it needs to be taught, to learn how to budget, because they've been used to eating those types of food anyway and to suddenly change – they should be taught how to buy cheaper nourishing food and make meals. The art has been lost – grandmother might have been able to do it – so what are they supposed to do? They can only do what they're used to doing and what they know. (Group of unemployed people, London)

Others pointed out that skills so long-lost will be difficult to re-acquire:

If there's nobody teaching us those skills, then it's very hard isn't it? We don't just have them, we learn them. (Young people's project)

A Beggar's Banquet

This man bilked the system — and public generosity. He claimed to be homeless and hungry yet lived a good life, driving a new £10,000 car. Andrew Malone tells a tale of our times.

The man who was in his early 20's, looked quickly around before lifting cardboard signs and plastic containers from the boot of the blue L registered hatchback. Then he changed into his work clothes: jeans and bomber jacket were swapped for a grubby sheepskin coat and an old duvet. He sat down near a busy subway and began playing his part with aplomb. Some office workers stopped to drop coins in the beggar's container moved by the sign on his chest: "Hungry and homeless please".

Sunday Times 20 February 1994

'PROFESSIONAL' BEGGING

Many participants thought 'professional' begging was rife. For example, there was this exchange between the project worker, talking first, and two older people:

I mean I think this article is talking about professional beggars, people who beg for a living. Do you think this happens?

That happens on a large scale.

Oh, yes. (Group of older people)

Many recalled stories about 'professional' beggars which they had seen in the media, especially in Sunday tabloids, for example:

They had that in London, he had a good job and he found that he could earn more in a day by standing begging and The News of the

World followed him. He went out of his Mercedes, went under the subway and changed his clothes. And he had a big house somewhere in London and he could earn up to £300 a day begging. (Group for low income families)

A member of a group of young people saw 'professional' begging as just the thin end of the wedge:

There's always been people who take advantage of other people's generosity hasn't there?

Many groups could not agree if 'professional' begging was a problem or not:

I don't think it's very common that you get begging professionally.

Well I disagree with you, you look at the story.

People that have expensive cars, you don't find them coming out in the street and begging.

Not rich people but people with nothing else to do.

But this is what the article is about, it's about people who have a brand new car who come out on the street and start begging. I mean for one thing they wouldn't actually get very far. They'd probably get a few pence to get home with for petrol but that's not going to get them very far in maintaining their car for instance, or doing anything. (Mental health service user's group)

BEGGING, STIGMA AND SOCIAL DIVISION

Most participants thought that poor people were often forced to beg and many participants said that they would give as much as their fixed incomes would allow. They felt that reports about 'professional' begging stigmatised all people who beg which, in turn, discouraged the public from giving money to people begging in order to survive:

I've done that, I think it was like that guy who has been accused of doing such things, of going 'round the corner, getting in a new car and driving off. I've seen him outside ASDA and felt sorry for the guy and I've said, 'Here mate, buy yourself a cup of coffee,' and it's probably the last quid I've had. (Group of disabled people)

It does happen in Glasgow but it's giving us a bad name. We beg for what we need to live on. But for these people, it personally is for their own ends, they have got a comfortable living compared to what the homeless people have, but they've got to get it. (A member of an anti-poverty youth group)

I mean today they are making it into a business a lot of them and this is what detracts from those people who actually need the help. You look at him and say, well, he could be living in a flat somewhere, nice home, and yet he's there begging, saying he's out of work, homeless, whatever, and you can't at first sight say whether he's right or wrong. I've given it to the lads who have sat in the subway with a card. I'll give him some money, but at the back of our mind you're thinking do they actually need it or are they working the system? (Another member of the group of disabled people)

Probably those people that are professional beggars, they've got more than anyone anyway. They just supplement what they've already got. People that are genuinely poor, that have to beg, that you see in the streets.

It's going to make people wary now.

It's going to make them look bad isn't it, so they won't get perhaps a cup of tea or a sandwich.

It's going to make people think, well is he a professional beggar? (Group of unemployed people, London)

Many people made the point that 'professional' beggars made it much more difficult for those in real need, such as homeless people, to supplement their inadequate incomes by begging. 'Professional' begging was thought to hit people in greatest poverty the hardest:

I agree with that statement because I've actually seen it happen. Why I disagree with that statement is because what it does is put people who are really in that homeless situation, that has no other alternative to begging, they then suffer because you do have people who have got more asking for money. (Group of lone parents, Bristol)

If people do this, other people are going to be less inclined to give to the poor anyway aren't they, because for fear that they're probably well off people with houses and cars. (Women's group)

Significantly, participants thought that a climate where there was mistrust of people begging would make poor people suspicious of each other. This woman thought that such division among poor people was a particular problem if a greater sense of solidarity was needed for effective anti-poverty campaigning. (see also Chapter 7)

> It's very important things like this, it puts the division. It divides the poor. It makes the poor fight between themselves. (Women's education project)

Some people thought that this backlash against begging was wrong when other people dishonestly make 'millions' and are not stigmatised in the same way:

> The ones we have to be afraid of and have the effect on society is not the people who beg at the bottom to increase their legal income by a few pounds. That's cheating in a way, but it doesn't hurt the state – but it hurts the state when people who make millions thwart the intention of so-called ethical government by lying, cheating, swindling and begging.

> No, but I mean if a lot of people start doing it, millions, the actual people who really need the money, taking their money, they're going to be losing out in the long run, beggars. (Group of young people)

THE MEDIA AND BEGGING

Most participants saw the media as being at the root of the negative image that begging has gained. People felt that media reporting tended to lump poor individuals together as a pathological group which affected how others saw them:

> Do you think people get tarred with the same brush, the ones that really need the money and the ones that do it professionally?

> They're tarred with the same brush but those in the money are deserving the tarring and the name they get. They are doing damage. (Group of older people)

Participants saw the media as instrumental in pathologising all forms of begging:

> I think what puts you off about beggars is that you've heard so much on the telly, so much from the actual papers that you just couldn't believe it. You think it's just a con for getting more money out of someone. (Group for low income families)

There was a general feeling that it was the media's exaggeration of the extent of 'professional' begging which caused many poor people to be stigmatised:

They're just really looking at one aspect, they're not looking at the background or anything are they? They're just taking one case and saying that all beggars are rotten people, basically. (Rural tenants group)

People felt that the media did this without thinking about its consequences or with any regard for people who need to beg as a means of survival. The same participant continued:

It might have been true in this case, maybe someone done it in this case, but they haven't reflected on the ones who are genuinely homeless who haven't or can't claim benefits because there is still people in that situation who can't. They haven't reflected on that sort of thing, they just took this one and blew it up, saying all beggars are the same. (Rural tenants group)

For many participants the crucial issue was that people begging because they had to, had been hit hard and unfairly by media reports:

But I feel sorry for them that are really in that situation, that are genuine, because they lost a hell of a lot of sympathy when that came out. They lost a hell of a lot and they just didn't deserve to lose it. (Group of unemployed people, Yorkshire)

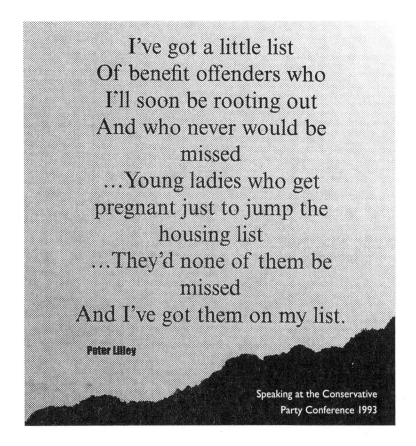

I've got a little list
Of benefit offenders who
I'll soon be rooting out
And who never would be
missed
...Young ladies who get
pregnant just to jump the
housing list
...They'd none of them be
missed
And I've got them on my list.

Peter Lilley

Speaking at the Conservative
Party Conference 1993

Peter Lilley's poem made many participants intensely angry:

> It's just crap, he doesn't live in the real world. (Group of lone parents, Yorkshire)

> Just pure ignorance, it's not even worth commenting on, just ignorance. (Lone parent's group, Glasgow)

> If I'd had known then what I know now, I wouldn't have got pregnant just to get my council house! My God, who's going to get pregnant and look after a bairn all them years just to get a council house? It's just totally idiotic. He's a pillock, he's a true pillock. (Group of unemployed people, Yorkshire)

Other people questioned the premise behind the minister's stigmatisation of single mothers. One participant asked if all single mothers, including middle-class single mothers, were becoming pregnant, just in order to jump the housing queue:

> So did Sarah Keayes [mistress of Conservative Government minister] get pregnant to jump the housing list? (Group of disabled people)

Some people, however, did think young women did become pregnant in order to obtain a home and said that they personally knew of cases where it had happened. There was, for example, this exchange between the project worker, speaking first, and some older people:

> *This article is talking about young girls who get pregnant to jump the housing list.*
>
> It's true.
>
> *Do you think that happens?*
>
> Yes, yes. As I said to you just now, they're above me, they get more from the Government than I get.
>
> Yes, yes.
>
> Yes certainly. (Group of older people)

There were similar comments from some young people:

> Yes that's true, young ladies do get pregnant just to jump the housing list.
>
> Yes, I know somebody who did that as well.
>
> She got pregnant so she could get herself a home. (Group of young people)

Others, like this unemployed claimant argued that statistically very few young single mothers obtain social housing:

> Despite every piece of work that's been done in terms of collecting information and facts, there are all these myths that there are hundreds and hundreds of young women who get pregnant just to get a council house – but every bit of research that has been done destroys the myths. (Group of unemployed people, Yorkshire)

Most participants, however, took a more pragmatic stance between these two positions arguing that sometimes young women might get pregnant in order to get housed, but more often they became pregnant for other reasons:

Most of them don't get pregnant, like, to jump the housing list, some are accidental. Maybe some of them do get pregnant so they can jump the housing list but not all of them do. (Young people's project)

People talked about the conditions which might lead a young woman to make such a decision. Most felt that it was understandable if young women became pregnant to escape appalling domestic circumstances. As one young man said:

The thing is we all know that there are women who do get pregnant to get on the housing list, and probably if I was a woman and I had nowhere to live, I would probably get pregnant to get a roof over my head. I look at it this way, supposing I had a mother and father, I have 5 brothers, 4 sisters and life was, literally, hell, shall we say in that house and I had to get out. Now, as a single young woman I would not be housed by the council, they'd basically turn me away ... I'd almost certainly get pregnant in order to get away from the social conditions I was living in. Rather than live on the street, it's far better to get pregnant and find somewhere to live that way. (Group of unemployed people, London)

I mean some people do think that a girl will get pregnant to get away from home because her life at home is so bad that they'll do anything to get away, so possibly, yes, they are doing. But they're doing it for a reason, not just so they can have a house and live on the state, they've actually got a lifestyle that they want to get away from. (Group of disabled people)

One woman spoke from personal experience:

I mean, I'm 28 now and he'll [her son] be two a week on Saturday and it's like the only reason I got pregnant was so that I could get out of my mum's because I can't get a house any other way at the end of the day. (Group for low income families)

Despite this, other people thought that young women would be ill-advised to become pregnant to escape bad conditions as the difficulties of caring for a child alone might, in fact, be greater than the problems they left:

You get a flat, you get more money, you'd have a kid 24 hours a day.

Oh yes, who's going to look after it? It's alright for you lot to say have a kid.

Yes, but some girls obviously prefer doing it that way.

Yes, that's true.

Some girls have kids just because they need something that they haven't had themselves. (Group of young people)

Any woman that gets pregnant just to get a house is living under a real delusion because you're giving yourself a life sentence of at least ten years. (Women's education project)

Other young women, like this member of a women's group in conversation with the project worker, might become pregnant because the local employment situation meant that there was no other way of gaining an income sufficient to leave home:

Because there's no jobs.

Did you get pregnant intentionally?

Yes.

SINGLE MOTHERS, GOVERNMENT AND 'BLAMING THE VICTIM'

Participants felt that the Conservative government had had to find a scapegoat for social problems such as crime and 'dependency' and that single mothers were an easy target:

I think they [the Government] just want to blame someone. I think they just wanted to blame them and that's what they've done. They blame the youngest and they just seem to want to put the blame on someone and the media find these young mothers that have got kids. (Group for low income families)

They're putting the blame on somebody.

Just like single parents. Everything at the moment is blamed on single parents.

Single parents are supposed to be a single woman that's gone out deliberately and got pregnant. They don't take into account the women that have been married or divorced – all sorts of reasons for being pregnant. (Group of lone parents, Yorkshire)

They've got to blame somebody and it's single parents' turn this time. It was miners ten years ago, it's single parents now. In ten years time it will be disabled people or old age pensioners. They just have to pick one certain group out of society to pick on every ten years. (Group of unemployed people, Yorkshire)

People also thought that politicians blamed the victim because they had little or no experience of what it is like to be poor themselves:

> But the key words are they're not in touch with reality, they don't know anything about reality, of course they don't. In fact, on the other side, I don't think we can even expect them to know about reality because they've never been there. John Major kept claiming he's been somewhere vaguely near it, but I don't think very near it. (LETS group)

This woman suggested that the stigma surrounding being a single mother was part of a divisive political campaign to reduce public spending on health and welfare:

> They want to take the money away, they want to take away the state's responsibility for raising children which is their responsibility in the same way as for education and for health care. And they want to say that these people are doing nothing and they deserve to die, because in this country, and in other countries, people aren't prepared to see families on the street dying of starvation and the Government wants to get it into people's minds that yes, that would be OK because it's their own fault and they bring it on themselves. And furthermore if you give them the chance they're going to cut your throat. So they're really trying to divide people up and brutalise people's attitudes. (Group of women involved in campaigns)

People believed that this political attack on single motherhood was supported by the media and the press in particular:

> They made a field day about this, it's politically fashionable. This is what is going to sell those papers. This is what people want ... they're going to build up this wee image, traditional values, we've done this, we've done that, this is wrong. All that shite going into the papers and they're blowing it right out of proportion, because that's what it was when this statement came out, it was all over the front pages for weeks or so. (Anti-poverty youth group)

Most groups saw government policy as the main culprit in reducing the life choices and opportunities of young women so that some might be forced into single motherhood. Many people argued that cuts in health and education spending hit single mothers hardest:

> Well why don't they put more money into the education system so
> that young girls have more options available and be educated? Why
> don't they put more money into the Health Service? (Group of lone
> parents, Bristol)

The sale of council houses was seen as creating another hardship for
single mothers needing accommodation:

> Well, I've never agreed with them selling council houses actually
> because council houses are for people that can't provide their own and
> all these people that they've bunged up and nine out of ten that have
> bought their own houses have had them repossessed and they're back
> on the council housing queue. (Group of disabled people)

In turn, the then Secretary of State for Social Security was seen as
blaming housing problems on the victims – single mothers:

> I think he's really blaming them for housing. I mean they're putting
> more pressure on somebody in a situation when they don't really need
> any pressure anyway because they've got enough to start with. That
> little list, in some way I think, God, my name's on the list you know.
> (Lone parent's group, Glasgow)

Some participants also related such attacks to political preoccupation
with the traditional family and traditional "family values":

> I mean if they cared at all like they say they do with all these moral
> values, it's actually better surely for a child who's in a disruptive
> household where the parents are fighting cat and dog and everything
> else. That has a much worse effect on the child than if they actually
> split up. It's sad that they've lost one parent, whichever it may be, but
> it's probably better for them in the long run hat they're living in a
> sounder household and a more peaceful household. whereas they're
> looking at textbook morals such as a family with two parents, mother,
> father, child per se. They're so tunnel-visioned about things. (Group
> of homeless people)

> And also we're supposed to stay in situations like with partners, like if
> your partner is violent, it doesn't matter as long as he's got the money
> as far as they're concerned. (Group of women involved in campaigns)

It is characterised by drugs, casual violence, petty crime, illegitimate children, homelessness, work avoidance and contempt for conventional values ... the underclass spawns illegitimate children without a care for tomorrow and feeds on a crime rate which rivals the United states in property offences.

Sunday Times 26 November 1989[1]

WHAT IS THE 'UNDERCLASS'?

There was a lot of disagreement about the idea of the 'underclass' conveyed by this article. Some participants saw society as being in a period of social and moral decay typified by the idea of an 'underclass':

> Yes, I think generally society is decaying into a complete underclass in a sense and these problems are there, not just for people who haven't got money but even for rich people. They're on drugs, they commit crime, big time crime. So although this is just petty crime, the chap with a bowler hat and a suit, he's committing big time crime – he's a bigger thief than a chap in petty crime. (Mental health service user's group)

Some people thought that the existence of an 'underclass' was a direct result of Conservative government policy:

> I think the Government has created the underclass, you know, they don't do it out of choice. (Lone parent's group, Glasgow)

Others of those who believed in the existence of an 'underclass' thought that it was created out of a class system in which people at the top tended to stigmatise those nearer the bottom:

> There shouldn't be, but there definitely is. 'I'm not interested in you', sort of thing. And a lot of people that are wrongly classed as the underclass are the salt of the earth. They do as much as they possibly can to help, others but they keep getting knocked down by higher income people. (Group for low income families)

> I think we're making it. There's definitely class distinction now, certainly a few years ago there wasn't – people were all equal. But they're not now, there is an underclass now. (Community centre users group)

Some, however, thought that the idea of an 'underclass' was exaggerated:

> I mean there is a certain element, but the vast majority of people in this area are honest, good, working – I mean maybe they're not working, but that's through no fault of their own – they're honest people. And it really bugs me that they class them because they come from this area that they must be an underclass, but there is a certain element of it. I mean if you're passing the chemist first thing in the morning you'll see drug addicts waiting at the chemist, I mean, you can't take that away, there is a certain element. (Group for low income families)

Others dismissed the notion of an 'underclass' more forcefully:

> Bollocks! (Women's education project)

Some people, like this member of a group of young people, were angered by the comparison made between Britain and America:

> That's a load of shit really, because he's from a totally different walk of life. You can't class America the same as Britain.

Many criticised the idea for what they saw as a very narrow, purely economic definition of an 'underclass':

> Under in relation to what? If you haven't got any money you're classified as an underclass by that very fact, but you may be perfectly not 'under' but very much 'over' in your ability to see the problems

and your capacity to appreciate beauty and joy and love and you can't do it because of lack of money. It's not an underclass at all. It's the distorted system which classifies people as 'under' or 'above', either way, it works both ways, the system of classification is foul, distorted and inhuman. (Group of older people)

Others saw some of the behaviours that the *Sunday Times* described as pathological as perfectly natural responses to poverty and marginalisation:

Petty crime? – if you're not getting what you need then you have to steal it. Illegitimate children?- if you do find another human unit who can give you some love and comfort. What it comes down to is two human units who haven't got enough money to buy any kind of contraceptives or maybe haven't gone to school properly so they haven't got the education to know what happens – illegitimate children. (Women's education project)

THE 'UNDERCLASS' AND YOUNG PEOPLE

People thought that the idea of an 'underclass' was especially harsh on young people, many of whom they believed had little hope:

See, I've struggled with my lad, he's 19 and he's at college and he lives on family allowance.

I thought at 17 I was going to change the world and I knew all there was. But who at that age could cope on their own?

We take all their dreams and take all their aspirations away from them. (Group of disabled people)

Some people, like this woman, thought that many of the things which the *Sunday Times* described were not pathological, but simply an attempt by young people to forge their own identities:

All the boys met because of the Mods and Rockers, and before that it was the Teddy Boys, it was exactly the same thing. Young people are finding their feet. Young people are kicking the traces. Young people need space to be able to find out who they are. (Women's education project)

This idea that the 'underclass' was being confused with wider youth culture was again raised here:

They're comparing in a sense to 'college drop-out people' of the 1960s, people we would have called hippies and beatniks in those days. (Group of homeless people)

Often young people are trying to create these identities from nothing:

> It's not as they're describing it. At the youth club we've got Asians and whites come in and it's the younger generation that have a lot of that attitude element. I can back that up to about a quarter because they haven't got the choice that we talked about earlier. And because of the poverty level that they've no spending money to buy their own entertainment. Now that they're pushed into this area and those that are evil-minded can get drugs supplies and, 'Look, I can vandalise this and it's given me half an hour entertainment'. They go on that path. And try to get them diverted from that path again needs financial backing. (Group of disabled people)

Another member of the same group saw education as a key way of achieving this diversion, but thought it required sufficient government support:

> But teaching a child right from wrong within society there used to be a special needs group where they came into school and sat down with a pupil and talked one-to-one. And they financed that and whether you're rich or poor, if you're in educational need, it should be there. Oh yes, yes. I think the standard of education has gone down and that's because the funds are not there. The Government is cutting back all over and yet they say they're not, so consequently some are going to suffer. And children are leaving school without an education, not able to get a job, and therefore they're drifting into this way of life. (Group of disabled people)

Most people saw the idea of a 'young' 'underclass' as another case of blaming the victim:

> These kids are actually the victims.

> That's right.

> Where I live in a multi-storey block there's families there, there is nowhere for those children to play ... Of course, they're going to be noisy, kids are noisy, boisterous. (Women's education project)

THE 'UNDERCLASS', CRIME, DRUGS AND GOVERNMENT

We saw in the previous chapter that people taking part in the project thought that poverty caused crime. Many believed that instead of just condemning such behaviour, government should act to tackle poverty. For example, this member of the group of women involved in campaigns said:

> Well even the police have recognised that people are having to steal because they haven't got any money. They're saying that the Government has made these problems and they're expecting the police to deal with them – but it's a political issue.

Some people saw crime as part of some young people's lives, but many objected to the way in which this was interpreted by the idea of the 'underclass'. This young participant again looked at the role of government in spreading the idea of an 'underclass' and reframing young people's lives and problems in terms of it:

> I suppose to a certain extent some of it is true because some young people's lives are characterised, I suppose, in a way by drugs because, again, peer pressure and stuff like that – it is just a part of life, do you know what I mean. But this work avoidance, 'illegitimate children': 'the underclass spawns illegitimate children' without a care for tomorrow and feeds on 'a crime rate which rivals the US in property offences'. Now that to me is a prick who's writing that and doesn't give a damn about the young people that are having to go through this in their everyday life under a regime which is actually supporting what is here. (Anti-poverty youth group)

Most people believed that drug use was more common among people with higher incomes who could afford to pay for their habits and that it was not widespread among poor people:

> I think it's a myth because when you look at people who are using drugs, you know, for example, a lot of the ones that are using drugs, they're the ones that can afford it, yes? (Lone parent, Bristol)

There was a feeling that poor people were stigmatised for alleged drug abuse and branded part of an 'underclass', while better off people could get away with such behaviour with little comment:

> There's rules for one and different rules for another.

> Well what about all these MPs that have got daughters that are drug

addicts? Well, it applies to them as well. (Group of older people)

A minority of participants thought that some poor people did take drugs as a psychological escape from poverty, but that this was ultimately self-defeating:

> The people that does drugs, they go out and spend all their money on drugs, I think it's their own fault.
>
> But a lot of the time don't you think that people get into drugs because of the state they're living in?
>
> Yes, but ...
>
> It's something to make them feel better because they're on the poverty line.
>
> Yes, but you get the drugs, you do the drugs and you've got to face it afterwards anyway, so they're worse off. (Young people's project)

This unemployed claimant agreed and made the point that government should look at the underlying causes of drug use and not just stigmatise users who are poor:

> People who take drugs whether it's alcohol, cannabis, heroin, even, they don't take them because they're happy, they take them because they're depressed. Now if the government was to help these people they should find out why they're depressed. It's obvious that people who've got no money, as we've discussed. poverty causes depression and many psychiatric illnesses. (Group of unemployed people, London)

Most participants, including this lone parent, thought that higher benefits might turn offenders on low incomes from committing crime:

> If they paid people a reasonable amount of money in benefits, some of the people that do commit a crime through poverty wouldn't have to commit these crimes so it would reduce the penal cost of court cases, judicial hearings, imprisonment so greatly that it would balance itself out and you'd have people more caring towards each other because they weren't worried about the stress of having to steal and maim people to survive, do you know what I mean? They wouldn't be caged animals. You'd be able to treat people better and feel better about yourself, within themselves. It's not cost-effective what they're doing. They're creating, spending more money and creating people to become criminals. (Group of lone parents, Glasgow)

THE 'UNDERCLASS' AND LONE PARENTS

Most people who took part in the project objected to the idea that lone parents, especially single mothers, were the cause of many of the problems included in the idea of the 'underclass':

> You've had unmarried mothers, you've always had crime, you've always had drugs. We've had these but they've come out more now than what they did before because there's more people that knows about them than what we ever did. (Women's group)

> When you look at the statistics most of the young offenders are from two-parent families, they're not from the single parents. (Group of lone parents, Yorkshire)

The 'underclass' argument was seen by some people as a campaign against lone parents as serious as other forms of oppression which they face:

> And this is part of the whole witch-hunt. I mean there was that big witch-hunt against single mothers very similar to this. You know, where they said single mothers were scroungers and our children are drug addicts and vandals and criminals. And therefore they whipped up a whole climate of hate against single mothers. And then they came in with the Child Support Act. You know so they can whip us. This kind of racism and sexism, and then they bring in laws so that they can beat us more. (Group of women involved in campaigns)

THE 'UNDERCLASS' AND LABELLING

Some people thought that labelling people as part of an 'underclass' could become a self-fulfilling prophecy:

> But don't you think this could be part of a self-fulfilling prophecy as well that these kids are growing up being told by society, 'You are the dregs. We don't want anything to do with you.' And they think, 'Well, if that's how you are going to treat me, why should I be any different?' And that's creating a section of society that has nothing to lose which is a very dangerous thing to do. (Group of disabled people)

Many believed that, once you were labelled as 'deviant' or as part of the 'underclass', it was incredibly difficult to shake off the stigma surrounding these labels:

Say you get somebody coming in to this centre that's been to prison and done his sentence, his sentence doesn't begin until he comes out of prison and he gets dogged every other way because he's been in prison. He's not allowed to be a normal person again: He's always labelled as a parasite or he won't work, he's workshy and this, that and the other. It's really weird how people pin labels on when they only know a quarter of the summary. (Group of lone parents, Yorkshire)

People saw media reports of the 'underclass' and poor people in general as perpetuating this process of labelling:

It's media coverage.

I don't like the word 'underclass'.

See I don't like the word 'grass roots', you know, when they say about 'grass roots' I always think it's something subterranean – there's nowt 'under' about me. (Women's education project)

Participants thought that many poor people, who had little other choice than to live in increasingly impoverished environments, where there was overcrowding and crime, were stigmatised by media amplification of the idea of the 'underclass':

The media blow it out of proportion. I mean there's always been an element of crime and violence in housing schemes throughout Britain. I mean we have so many people, I mean, at one time. If you'd taken _____ [local social housing estate] on its own, it's pre-fabs. You've got multi-stories and you've got maybe 80-odd families in a high block of flats, and at one time there was only a few families lived in that. And you've got your crowd, and you have it – there always has been and there always will be. But I think the media do now blow it completely out of proportion. (Group for low income families)

It's propaganda put out by people that have got jobs. Lords and these MPs that talk out saying that, 'Well, he's just a dole scrounger.' They don't know what it is. Let's face it, you'll not hear anybody 'round here calling anybody the underclass because they're all in the same bloody boat. (Group of unemployed people, Yorkshire)

THE MEDIA

As well as commenting on the four articles, some groups, when time permitted, also talked about the role of the media in reporting poverty more generally. Many people believed that the negative images of poor people presented in the press perpetuated poverty, by creating and reinforcing negative attitudes among the general public:

> But it's the media that portray that stereotype and then the general public pick up on that and then it feeds in to the system and then people start believing bullshit. (Group of lone parents, Bristol)

Some participants saw such stereotyping as a way of sensationalising poverty; and that such sensationalism – especially by the press, and by the right of centre press particularly – was used to attract bigger markets:

> I think we always feel we don't understand. It's like reporting several large creatures with five legs roaming around the streets of Surrey. Now even if people don't believe it's there they'll still buy the newspaper because it's something sensational, it's different. And when you write about the underclass, illegitimate mothers, children taking drugs, etc., it's something that people in The City, or people that are upper class, middle class, they fear it, they don't understand, so they buy the paper to try and see this world's that existing that shouldn't exist. I don't really think that when they buy papers and read the article they really care – it's a curiosity value. It's what are these creatures, these strange beings of the underclass who take drugs and I think that's actually what it is, they're people who are dehumanised. When the term is underclass, that is the curiosity. (Group of unemployed people, London)

This exchange between a group of older people, conveys the feeling of many participants that the press preys on the emotions of their readership to maintain sales, even if reports are distorted:

> Well, I think they're feeding on the emotions of people all the time, people's emotions sell newspapers.
>
> They're very clever at it – very psychologically adept.
>
> You're right.
>
> All they're interested in is circulation but basically they don't give two hoots about the people they're writing about and neither do they give

two hoots about the accuracy of their comments as a succession of libel writs against a certain batch of the press has proved. Unfortunately the poor person in the street can't sue for libel because there's no legal aid for libel action. If there was such a thing as legal aid for libel action you can bet your bottom dollar that the press reports about poverty would very soon moderate. (Group of homeless people)

Many participants questioned the political partiality of the press. For example:

And also depending what paper it is, different newspapers have different political leanings which is another ridiculous situation really if we've got a free press. (Group of homeless people)

And they're just sticking up for the Government, because they want to keep the Government in power. They don't see the facts, they just see what the Government wants them to see and what they want to see. (Community centre users group)

NOTES

1 The *Sunday Times*, 'The British Underclass', News Focus: Opinion editorial, 26 November 1989.

SUMMARY

- Participants rejected media stereotypes of poor people as lacking initiative and budgeting skills and highlighted the problems of maintaining a healthy diet and lifestyle on low incomes and inadequate benefits.
- Participants were divided over media reports of 'professional' begging. There was agreement amongst most participants that it did exist, but to nothing like the extent portrayed by politicians or the media. The effect of such reports was seen as divisive, discouraging people from giving money to beggars and lumping together and stigmatising all poor people and people who beg, as potentially fraudulent.
- Anger was the overriding reaction of participants to ministerial statements about young women becoming pregnant in order to jump the housing queue. Opinion was divided over whether this happened. The general opinion was that appalling domestic and economic situations might make this the only option for a small number of young women. Some participants believed that governments had scapegoated young single mothers in order to divert attention from problems arising from its own housing policies and that sympathetic sections of the media colluded in this.
- There was little agreement among poor people in the project about whether there was an 'underclass' in Britain and little support for the concept. The assumptions embraced in the idea about lone parents, young people, drugs and crime were mostly rejected. Many participants believed that poverty drove people into crime. Many viewed the idea of the 'underclass' as damaging and some as counter-productive.
- Most people in the project expressed strong feelings about the media. Many believed that the negative images of poor people presented by the media perpetuated poverty by creating and reinforcing negative attitudes among people more generally.
- Media reporting of poverty was frequently seen as sensationalist to attract interest. Press reporting particularly, was seen as biased to the political right.

7 Taking action on poverty

In this chapter we set out people's ideas and proposals for tackling poverty. The discussion focused on two related areas; first, what participants thought could be done to reduce poverty and disadvantage; and, second, what part people with experience of poverty might play in anti-poverty action. People were as keen to explore solutions to poverty as they had been to identify the causes and many had a lot to say. Participants were enthusiastic and committed; but also realistic about the prospects for change.

This chapter first presents poor people's views about their own involvement, before turning to their proposals for reducing poverty.

INVOLVING POOR PEOPLE

Most participants believed that anti-poverty action should involve people with experience of poverty. Three quarters of the groups who took part thought that poor people should have a say in debates about poverty. Most participants raised this issue before we had even asked them specifically about it. They felt that a voice had constantly been denied poor people in the past, and was still denied them in the present:

> We'd like to be heard. (Women's group)

> People should be able to give over their point of view, their ideas, whether their ideas are adopted in whole or in part, because everybody's situation is different. (Group for low income families)

Yes, through telly. They have their say, everybody else in Government, everybody else has their say, but you don't always get enough of our side. (Group of lone parents, Yorkshire)

Many people thought that the involvement of poor people in anti-poverty initiatives was a matter of principle. They argued that decision-making processes should not be taken away from the people who were most affected by their outcomes:

Well, we are the ones affected so we should be centrally involved in deciding how resources are allocated because it's us. It's our lives so we should decide.

We're the ones affected.

They should be accountable to us, we should be able to ask them questions and get the answers. (Group of women involved in campaigns)

People thought that the lack of consultation by authorities with poor people concerning anti-poverty action, further marginalised them. Older people had a lot to say on this issue, for example, this older man who was active in anti-poverty campaigning, in an exchange with the project worker:

We need a voice. We need the care. As you get older you need more and more care and you're entitled to that and you should get it. But you need a voice, you're not a fool when you get old. Some people will deteriorate, but it's surprising how active a person's mind can be. And not only active but they have the knowledge and the experience, and youth wants that experience. Until the last hundred years, say, and it still is existing in other parts of the world, the aged people, the grandparents have a voice. They're referred to, they're revered and their experience counts. They've cast us aside. 'Oh, we've got to look after ourselves. I suppose we could let them perish, put them in a home, give them a minimum and hope they peg out pretty soon'. But you need their experience, youth is exuberant, it's got the vitality, it hasn't got the experience. it doesn't want the experience currently.

So should older people be speaking out about poverty and discrimination?

They should be allowed a voice even with, unfortunately, the deterioration of old age, there's still an active, knowledgeable and powerful voice accessible to the public and never sought. (Group of older people)

People felt that this lack of discussion with poor people led them to feel that they had no control over anti-poverty action:

> Because they're not asked. If you look at it in another way, it's the same thing that's happening to disabled people, because you get the able-bodied people suggesting what is better for the disabled people so they don't ask the disabled people and they're doing exactly the same thing with the poor. They're saying, 'Well, this should keep them going. They should be able to live on forty quid a week', but they don't actually ask them if they can survive on that amount of money. (Group of disabled people)

Many participants thought that if their voice was to be effective a large number of poor people would need to be involved:

> I think doing it in numbers, safety in numbers. If you're going to do anything about it then do it in numbers and then you're not singled out by people who go 'Oh, she's a trouble-maker'. (Group of lone parents, Yorkshire)

> I mean I think if we can help each other, if we can come here and we can talk to each other and give each other spirit. (Women's education project)

> Just enable them to get together, just know the fact of what you're doing. (LETS group)

Such first steps were seen as an important factor both in effective campaigning and towards personal empowerment by another member of the group:

> Once people begin to realise that they can do things and have some control over their everyday lives then they'll begin to think about what the hell are we doing in this life anyway? (LETS group)

He stressed the importance of remembering the lessons to be learned from personal experience of poverty when people get involved in anti-poverty action:

> My main thing, my main thing personally that I think is important to get across, is basically if you get involved in poverty with direct experience of it don't forget the lessons you've learned. Once you've become unpoor again, if you're one of those who dip out of poverty from relatively quick chunks of life, don't forget, bring the positive stuff out of it, and try to do something about it and retain it and keep it

with you and keep empathy with people that have even been more deserving than you have when you're going through it personally, because there's always somebody worse off. The key factor is there's always somebody out there a damn sight worse off than you are and everybody knows that, or most of the people I talk to, that I know, because I don't personally know people who live under bridges. Learn the lessons and keep them and do something about it, make some use of it, if you know that you will see the end of poverty in a certain amount of time. (LETS group)

TAKING PART IN ANTI-POVERTY CAMPAIGNS

Participants saw campaigning by poor people for a voice for poor people as an essential first step towards being heard. Some had been politically active, or had taken part in anti-poverty campaigning and often viewed such campaigns as ad hoc and disorganised, but still of value:

> We're getting up and fighting ... We went to Westminster and we went into lots of job centres and that the day before and we said, 'We're not working for workfare. We want proper jobs with proper pay', and believe me, there were an awful lot of people there and they weren't negative. (Women's education project)

> We do our bit, we do our bit, and it's fragmented, everything's a bit here and a bit there and a bit all over the place.

> So what do you do ... you can't sit back and do nowt. (Women's education project)

People held what they considered to be realistic views of campaigning. It was not seen as a panacea. Many had discouraging personal experiences of campaigns which they had been a part of, for example:

> Campaigned for the benefit didn't I in '91. We did a fabulous campaign for under-five discrimination in mobility allowance and we even took a coach full of disabled kiddies down to the parliament and it went really well – but it still didn't change their minds. An MP said she would meet us and when we got there she said she'd meet two of the mothers and Andy who was welfare Rights worker. And no kids, because she says, 'well, under-fives, they can't walk properly anyway'. I don't know where she's been living. She said they don't need to be mobile under-fives. I said kids start school at three these days, you know nursery – they've got to walk. But she had no concept at all of

what it's like bringing a child up, never mind a disabled child. (Group of unemployed people, Yorkshire)

WHY PEOPLE HAVE NOT BEEN ACTIVE IN CAMPAIGNS

People gave numerous reasons why in the past many poor people had not been active in anti-poverty campaigning. One reason was that people would not want to be identified with poverty:

People don't want to class themselves as poor, some people. (Lone parent, Glasgow)

But your feeling is that some people wouldn't, they wouldn't want to be seen as poor?

That's right, and they wouldn't want to admit it to other people, not that they wouldn't want to admit it to themselves. (LETS group in conversation with the project worker)

Another reason was that the continual marginalisation poor people face made them pessimistic about the success of such campaigns:

Because they're always getting knocked back aren't they. Always saying that people on low incomes or benefits – quite basically, some of these Conservatives think we are the scum of the earth and we should be shot. I mean it does put a lot of people off, they say what the hell, why bother, we haven't got a chance. (Rural tenants group)

Participants thought that others did not want to become involved for fear of retribution:

What does get said gets turned around and used against us. (Women's group)

There was particular fear of retribution by the DSS:

They're just scared, they don't get involved with things. I think they're just scared of reprisals from the DSS, a lot of them, as well. I mean if they've got to go and see DSS a lot of them are really scared, they don't like to fight, they're scared of authority. If you go to DSS you go and sit across from a man in a suit and it just scares people and a lot of them are scared of reprisals.

… It's like rallies, they're afraid to be seen.

Seen? By the DSS?

Well, they spy on you don't they? (Group of unemployed people, Yorkshire)

It could then be difficult to involve people:

What about the Child Poverty Action Group. We've been involved with them, that day, and nobody turned up for their meeting. (Women's group)

The marginalisation felt by many participants, with the subsequent feelings of powerlessness, made people's lack of involvement in campaigns understandable to participants:

Yes, because they don't have a voice and they're down at the bottom and they've probably no way of expressing themselves to anybody. (Group of disabled people)

Also when you're living on benefits, on a low income, and you're struggling to survive on a daily basis, you're self-esteem gets low and if you haven't got much confidence you're not likely to shout about poverty. I mean you're not likely to sort of say it's terrible living on this much money. You feel very isolated, you haven't got the confidence to speak up. And, organisations like ours, we can go and do outreach and talk to people, make them see that they're not the only one in this situation, that there are people that understand, but it's very limited what we can do. (Group of lone parents, Bristol)

However reluctance to get involved was not seen to be confined to just poor people, or associated only with poverty. It was noted in all sections of society:

But a lot of people don't want to get involved anyway. If you think of people in work, in trade unions, I mean how many people come forward to the shop stewards? Very few. How many people attend branch meetings? Very few. So it isn't just like people who are unemployed who don't want to get involved, you'll find it anywhere, in all walks of life. (Group of unemployed people, Yorkshire)

This homeless person thought that providing suitable opportunities for people to get together to work out what they would do, could overcome this problem:

Yes, they should be involved and, yes, they should be listened to, but you need to get the interest of the people who are really in that situation because often they're too busy struggling and living an existence to actually take part, and they are very cynical about whether anybody's going to listen so they don't think it's worth it. And if you can motivate them to do it, you've got to develop a structure about how you're going to use what they say – there has to be a lot of thought put in to it. I think it's very good groups here or a group in Manchester and a group in Scotland meeting once a week like, putting together what people have to say. Perhaps that's a start. (Group of homeless people)

Some participants thought that many poor people might not want to get involved because of the time and energy required. Day-to-day life and campaigning were not always seen to sit comfortably together and this was not necessarily to do with being poor:

Yes, but don't expect that everybody will have that energy that you have now because mine's been spent in all sorts of directions.

But you're doing something, that's the point I'm making, you're doing your bit as well.

Yes, but in the end sometimes you think do I have to care, whatever I'm doing, it's like do I save the world and lose the family?

Sometimes you need a rest for yourself.

It isn't only that, you need a life for yourself too. I've spent so much of my life living bits of other people. I need a life for me.

That's what I mean. For me the government took that, and most of the time I couldn't give a toss what they're doing because there's nothing I can do to change it. Yes I can join, I've done it in the past, and at the end of the day there's me too you know. (Women's education project)

People also talked about the off-putting effects of the problems and difficulties associated with conventional campaigning and schemes for involvement:

As I mentioned before – the over 50s group who are trying to do so much for themselves because nobody seems to want any of them anymore. They don't have a building and they see a building – 'Yes,' they said, 'OK, you don't have a building get a building'. When they get a building they tell them there's no money, so where do you start? Where do you end?

And also there is no point having a consultation if then the people have no control over how resources are allocated. Councils have had consultation with disabled people and carers, but when it comes to your assessment for services you have no say over what services you have to get. So just consultation without decision-making on where the resources go is just a cosmetic exercise. (Group of women involved in campaigns)

'POVERTY RIOTS'?

Some participants saw the future in terms of more demonstrations and direct action by poor people:

Well are they going to the Government and saying, 'Well look'?

Well they will eventually, they'll all rise up won't they, like the disabled are now, fighting for their rights. The poor will rise up and say, 'Look, we've had enough of this'. It's not going to go on indefinitely. One of these days there's riots here, there and everywhere, it's not going to just be racial riots, it's going to be poverty riots isn't it? It's going to happen, you see it happening. (Group of disabled people)

This group of women involved in campaigns felt that the economic and social divisions which government policy created, including divisions among poor people, made it more difficult to challenge it:

But it suits the Government to have those divisions in the black community as well. Every community since then [1979] has those divisions – while you're fighting each other you're not fighting them.

For this homeless person, the issue was still to get poverty on to the political agenda:

Well, I'm tempted to comment on the classic poverty debate on the individual level – the poor man says to the rich man, I'm very poor, all I can afford is this stocking-mask and gun, 'Hand it over!' But that's a little bit cynical. What has to done on the poverty debate is to find an area which those are in a position to make policy, whereby they are forced to sit up and listen. Am I saying the revolution must start now? Well, maybe, maybe not, but it will not be addressed until the policy makers begin to recognise that poverty exists which at present they don't. (Group of homeless people)

ACCOUNTABILITY AND REPRESENTATION

As well as talking about poor people's involvement through campaigning and direct action, participants highlighted the need for accountability and representation. Many believed that policy makers should be made more accountable for their actions to poor people:

> Yes, I think not so much the poor campaign, I think what should happen is these ministers and the secretaries of state should come to us before they make these daft remarks. They should have an audience in front of them and then they should think to themselves, would I make such a remark if I was in front of 200, 500, 600 unemployed or low income people, or beggars. And that gentleman that was supposed to be treading on the homeless when he came out of the opera, if he'd had a hall filled full of homeless people he wouldn't have said that remark. So they're clearly out of touch with the people they're referring to. They need to come to us, not us to them, they need to come to us.

> Well, it's like a statement like Marie Antoinette was saying 'Let them eat cake' if they have no bread, they've got as much understanding of that. I think we should be given a slot on television like these politicians, to put our point over.

> See you automatically believe that if someone has been to Eton or Cambridge or Oxford they're intelligent, but I mean the best scholars aren't always the wisest men. (Group of unemployed people, London)

Many discussions developed the issue of poor people being represented by poor people:

> Don't allow ministers to be eligible for a seat, put out a local person or votes for local people that have experienced first hand things to be able to sit in these seats. (Member of Lone parent's group, Glasgow)

> More people involved with first hand experience. (Rural tenants group)

Participants generally argued that poor people should be present on all decision-making bodies which affected aspects of the lives of poor people:

> I think that people who live in poverty should be adequately represented like in housing committees, benefits advisers, everywhere, anybody that ever needs to discuss poverty.

> *All the statutory agencies?*

Yes, everybody. There should be forums which include people who live in poverty, single parents, homeless people, whatever their situation is, it should be made up of representatives and multi-racial groups. (Group of lone parents, Bristol)

I was going to say it would be good like if there was a place within government, be it local or central, where there was a citizens' forum, like central government, I suppose, where there was that constant input from people who really live these lives. (Group of lone parents, Glasgow)

People thought that it was important for policy makers to know what it was like to be poor. Some thought that politicians should be made to live on a low income for a period:

Yes, sit there until they talk to you. Or kick them out and see what they say.

Let them live on the streets.

Make sure it's snowing.

Let all the presidents and all them lot, let them live on the streets and see how they square up. (Young people's project)

Others thought that the results were likely to be misleading:

They should come and live here and see what it's like.

Yes, but they do that, for a week or a month. They don't do it for years and get into debt.

We had that television programme here.

Yes, for a week.

That MP did it, his family didn't.

They do a thing and they put it on telly and they turn it 'round.

Yes, say, 'Oh, they should be able to survive on what they've got'. (Women's group)

STARTING LOCALLY

Participants thought that poor people needed strength in numbers if they were to influence national poverty debates and developments. Most people believed that for this to happen and for initiatives to be effective, they should be locally based. All the groups who were actively involved who took part in the project, were locally based. But they also saw a natural process of networking and information sharing as the most effective way of involving poor people in anti-poverty action:

> By networking throughout the country we're going to get our strength. (Women's education project)

> Networking between like districts, within your district and between districts. Information basically is power. If you don't have the information you can't take action … so definitely we need to share information with as many people as possible with a local agenda. You need to get people there, sit down and organise a piece of the action. What you also need is the assistance and support for the services and agencies not only for yourself through the work that you prepare but also to train others that want to become involved and train them to empower themselves and take action on what they want to do with regards to poverty locally. (Anti-poverty youth group)

In this youth group's locality, such initiatives are supported by an anti-poverty resource pack produced by a regional umbrella organisation to provide information and contact addresses of relevant agencies to people particularly vulnerable to poverty.

While groups emphasised the importance of local initiatives involving poor people, they weren't in a position to develop the idea in more detail. Some groups saw poor people's self-help and mutual aid initiatives as a key route both to involving more people with experience of poverty and to enabling them to take part in poverty debates and developments. This participant talked about how setting up a LETS (Local Exchange Trading System) scheme could help. As we have said, members of LETS exchange goods and labour without using money. Instead a mutual non-cash exchange involving a mixture of goods and services is arranged:

> I think one thing that we can do as a group to help, is like setting up a LETS scheme to allow people who live in the same area to share services they can provide in order to come out of the poverty trap and I think that would be of use. (Mental health service user's group)

A member of a LETS thought that locally-based centres where cheap food and leisure facilities were available would provide support and a sense of community in deprived areas as well as combat poverty:

What came into my mind when you said that was to be able to have a centre, like in towns and villages for people, because there aren't the social services that were sort of available once, supposedly in order to help poverty – in order to help people just in their daily lifestyle. A kind of community centre for people where there could be for instance a play area for children, a cafe, a grocery shop, lectures. (LETS group)

BROADER ACTION AGAINST POVERTY

In addition to seeing the involvement of people with first hand experience of poverty as an essential part of all anti-poverty practice and policy, participants identified a range of other proposals for how poverty should be tackled. All involve government. These proposals can be grouped into three main categories:

- General government policy: including overall strategies and commitment to reduce poverty;
- Government social policy: including reform of benefits, housing, child support and child care policy;
- Government employment policy: including job creation, education, training and investment.

We will now look at these in turn.

GENERAL GOVERNMENT POLICY

CHALLENGING POLITICAL INDIFFERENCE TO ANTI-POVERTY ACTION

Many participants thought that to be effective on a national scale, anti-poverty initiatives needed political backing, preferably by the government of the day:

> Those in power should have goodwill. Goodwill is necessary, both at the top and the bottom and at the moment, especially at the top. It's conspicuous by its absence. There are a few, but they haven't got the power, the vast majority suppress them and do what they usually do for themselves. (Group of older people)

People shared the view that politicians were motivated by self-interest. Most participants blamed successive Conservative governments for directly causing poverty. Many believed that *all* political parties were indifferent to poor people and anti-poverty action:

It won't make any difference if Labour got in because they're not going to stop anything that John Major already _____ up. It would take the amount of time what it's taken to ___ it up like they have done anyway, like the Tories – it's going to take double that amount to rectify it with another government.

Do you think politicians want to rectify it?

No. They're in it just for the money.

They just want their wages at the end of the day.

They're all in it to make money, same as what the unemployment people do, try doing. Trying to make money, extra money, and that's what they're trying to do, and anyway, they can do it, even if it's screwing like about a thousand people, they'll do it. (Group of young people in conversation with the project worker)

Despite this common mistrust of the political process, government investment was still seen as a major way of ameliorating poverty:

I think there's been a lack of investment in the infrastructure, housing, probably the roads. I mean some spending that can create work. You've had massive homelessness and a reduction in house building and most building workers, so an investment in house builders – that helps. (Group of unemployed people, Yorkshire)

INITIATIVES FOR INVESTMENT

Some participants thought that there would only be effective investment if the process by which money was allocated was reformed. For example, schemes like City Challenge, providing grants for urban regeneration could lead to the creation of jobs in depressed areas, but the process by which this money was obtained and used was seen as inefficient and unclear:

Well, instead of just directing the City Challenge money to _____ [a suburb] get it so it benefits all of _____ [the city].

What's that?

City Challenge? It's money –

Money which is brought into the city to help with certain elements like poverty and so on and to establish places of work and so on, so it gives people a chance to actually get into the work environment and to help them with certain needs.

And people have to put a bid in, a tender, to get this. Instead of the money, it was a lottery because everybody put in a tender to the Minister and he decided where it went. (Group of disabled people)

People saw the best way of raising money for extra investment to be through increased personal taxation, especially increases in income tax:

> When the question was asked would workers be prepared to pay an extra three pence a week in tax, or three pence in the pound in tax to keep the National Health Service in good order, most people agreed to that. they thought it was a great idea, but the government didn't take it up and in the mean time they're closing down hospitals right, left and centre. (Group of disabled people)

Some participants believed that the reallocation of resources, for example from defence to social security, was essential in the fight against poverty:

> The diversion of resources away from Trident and such like. I think that's an absolute priority when you think of the millions of pounds that are going into that daily. (LETS group)

Some participants were pessimistic about the level of investment that could be mobilised in the future. They saw responsibility lying with government but were doubtful whether future governments would accept it and put right the mistakes that their predecessors had made:

> Well we've got this great divide with all statistics getting bigger rather than smaller. But without droning on about that ... it's the will to do something about it which the politicians don't seem to have. I think politically there are certain issues in society that shouldn't be a question of party politics, something as basic as living standards and because there are people to address such problems there should be all-party groups to address these things and come up with solutions and I think it's the long term policy of government ... Governments present and past have never had the foresight to see that that [unemployment] was obviously going to happen at some point and to think about what they're doing now in retrospect after the problems have happened, to relocate and redevelop areas. they should know by their mistakes and actually plan much further ahead with their policies to where employment is going to be and what it's going to be and also the fact that the population is basically a lot bigger ... But if the system is there to help people with problems but sooner or later there's going to be

more people, twice as many taking money out of the system as there are putting in, but that doesn't mean they're wrong, it's the government's responsibility to the whole of society to get that right and balance it out. But will it ever happen because it's their own self-interest? I mean those that pretend to be in power are those earning the higher salaries. (Group of homeless people)

The same participant thought that the way to 'balance it out' was through: *'Redistribution of wealth'*. But others thought this proposal was unlikely to be implemented.

GOVERNMENT SOCIAL POLICY

GOVERNMENT AND INCOME MAINTENANCE

Most people thought that the welfare benefits system needed urgent reform if poverty was to be tackled. Many urged that benefit levels should be raised as a priority. This exchange between the project worker and a woman on benefits was typical:

I mean you do need more basic day to day things, better resources and things like that – and more money. You need more money.

So you're talking about, in the immediate anyway, having higher benefits, is that what you mean?

Yes, higher benefits. (Group of women involved in campaigns)

Older people were especially angry at what they regarded as the derisory amount they received from state pensions. They felt particularly bitter that pensions had not kept pace with earnings. They wanted this to be rectified immediately. One older person, talking about the pensioners' campaign to raise pensions led by Jack Jones, said:

And he's very good about talking on behalf of pensioners and poverty and so on. And he was the one who said if they had pegged the pension, the amount of money he gave, to the inflation. If they had just done that we would have been what oh well, over £70.00 better off. (Group of older people)

As we saw in Chapter 4, many people viewed the introduction of the Child Support Agency to enforce child maintenance payments as an additional cause of poverty. Many lone parents argued for the urgent reform of the child support policy:

If we could put over our view and say that the Child Support Agency policies should be changed because they're causing a lot of problems between couples that could first of all get back together ... they say 'oh right, we want you to pay £135 a week for your kids. You've got another family, another marriage. You've maybe got four kids or five, you've got to keep them off the same wage – you can't do it. (Group for low income families)

However some people felt powerless to act against the bureaucracy of the Child Support Agency:

How can I fight them? What can I do? I can't reach them ,it's now being sent. But I'm due for my next month's in a week's time. How long is that going to take before that comes? ... It's all gone, I've got nothing. (Women's education project)

THE GOVERNMENT AND HOUSING

Another area of reform to tackle poverty which participants identified was housing:

A good way to create more jobs is to build more houses, it's like a service industry. So you're getting people off the streets into work by building houses, getting people off the streets that are homeless and money's going to the council for the houses, for paying rent, so it's just a big circle where money's changing hands, we'd be better off if you can understand what I mean. (Women's group)

This problem of providing affordable housing cropped up in many discussions. Many groups felt that legislation should be changed to reintroduce the public provision of low cost social housing:

Yes it's a simple change in the law to let councils to again be house providers because that's been taken away from them. Because at the end of the day councils or the government, either local or central government, are the best providers of good quality, low cost housing. The private sector isn't interested, never has been. Private rented aren't interested. Private rented housing is minimum now, apart from bedsits.

Well, my main problem is I've got all the kids wanting to find flats and they are bedsits, like one room, but they're wanting £125 bonds [deposits]. There's no proper flats provided for single young workers. There's plenty for the elderly and the handicapped but not for the young'uns.

And if they're on income support they won't take bonds so they can't take flats now because they can't raise the money for bonds. (Group of unemployed people, Yorkshire)

Some people saw the re-implementation of rent controls to provide affordable housing in the private sector as another priority:

Well central government erected a system of controls which government has now been dismantled. And Rachmanism is coming back, there's distinct evidence in that direction … Small things could help like rent levels having ceilings on them.

Well there are as far as housing benefit is concerned.

Yes, but ceilings on them which the landlords can charge. They'd be more likely to take people on benefits then, it would be easier to get accommodation.

Well that's what rent control is about isn't it?

They don't have rent control anymore, they took it away.

That's what I mean, rents have been decontrolled. (Group of homeless people)

GOVERNMENT AND CHILD CARE

Many people, particularly lone parents, identified the need for the provision of low cost child care to make it possible for them to find employment and come off benefits:

Proper child care, quality child care.

… The child care situation as well because you're trapped in poverty, you want to get out of poverty to go and find a job but there isn't proper child care or an adequate quality child care available for people on low income or people in poverty so that they can get out of that situation. Therefore you're frustrated and it's that kind of trap. (Group of lone parents, Bristol)

Well if we had enough child care, we'd have a few more jobs wouldn't we? Well, yes, get more jobs in child care, yes. Because as a single parent not having child care is a big downside – you rely on yourself if you've not got a family 'round the corner, you've got nobody. You can't go out after school-time, well, after bed-time, you can't go anywhere. In the school holidays if you have a job what do you do? If you've to work at weekends you can't work at evenings. You can't work at weekends, you can only work in school terms and hope the kid's not poorly. So if you take a job on you've got to think about all this. And if you go for a job and you mention you're a single parent, they're going to have to do all this, well how would you go on in school holidays because they don't want to take somebody on who might put in sick for a couple of weeks in school holidays. So it's against you that you're a single parent for getting a job if you've got kids. (Group of lone parents, Yorkshire)

I don't think women should be forced to go back out to work if they want to stay at home and be with their children, but I think all women and all children, more to the point, in the interests of children, should get a decent pre-school education or nursery or whatever to give their parents the opportunity to go out to work. These places, places for children, are not there in nursery schools either in the public or in the private sector so people can't go out and contribute something to society even if they want to. (Lone parent's group, Glasgow)

One lone mother was critical of child care provision which was restricted to families seen as 'dangerous' or 'dysfunctional'. She felt that there should be universal provision:

When I became a single parent I applied to put Sharon in there [a local nursery] and they asked me if I took drugs and I said no. They asked me if my child was abused and I said no. And they said, no I'm sorry, we can't help you, we can't help you go back to work. (Group for low income families)

GOVERNMENT AND TRAVEL AND LEISURE

Earlier in the book, poor people talked about the stress and emotional problems caused by poverty and the importance of leisure to relieve them. Some suggested here that affordable 'travel and leisure' should be provided by government for people on low incomes:

One other thing that has to be done as well, travel and leisure have to be made available to people in poverty to try and relieve the pressure. People need something to switch off to from poverty, so it seems a daft thing, but the way society is nowadays and the lives that people in poverty live there's no recreation. We need to look at this side of things, we need to develop these services for gearing people that are going through these experiences what they need to cope. Not just be happy yes, we've got a great leisure centre, but just to cope with the depression and the stress that they have to go through when they're living in poverty. And if we can give them the access to the services which can help, not only social work and community education and all the rest of it, but if we can look at the leisure side of things, leisure and recreation, we can potentially have one like that because people have got all day, they've got all night in poverty, they get so pissed off staying in the house for twenty-four hours a day. (Anti-poverty youth group)

I think that another thing they ought to do is with people with families try and give them holidays because I think you need to get away and if there was some organisation because the stress that you're all under. I mean even if they're like one-parent families with cheap caravan holidays. I think that's essential. (Group of unemployed people, London)

There should be better respite care for people, for people that want to go abroad for breaks, there should be things to pay for them, access for them to go and return back in their community with a more better, fresh mind, you know. Because you're in a rut with everything keeping you down and you do need certain holidays to bring you back because, after all, that's what they do. Because they do it and come up with all these ideas to keep us down, so why can't we go away and come back to help them – to say, 'Listen, now my mind is as clear as yours'. We ought to live much better, there's no need for you living in an, I don't know the right word. You know it seems very lean to me – one set of people can get the break to make them more healthier, and the other lot can't get that sort of break. It's not right. (Women's group)

GOVERNMENT EMPLOYMENT POLICY

CREATING EMPLOYMENT

Almost all participants thought that investment in job creation was needed. A member of a women's group put it simply:

Create more jobs.

One lone mother argued that investment in employment was needed especially urgently in deprived areas like her own:

I can't even find a job that doesn't suit me. I think out of all the things, I've had one reply back. My son the other week put in 70 job applications and he got one reply out of that. He got the job and then was told he couldn't have the job because the funding had run out. And yet you've got the pressure on you that you've got to go out and find a job. But if they're manufacturing jobs then they're only going to last for six months or nine months, that's crueller in some ways than letting you stop on benefit. (Group of lone parents, Yorkshire)

People thought that investment in employment was needed for all groups, including young job-seekers:

Yes I mean it's not even just like for example with the teenagers, there's people in this area that I know, one or two who are about 28, 29, that have applied for jobs and they're told they're too old. I mean what hope is there for them in the future? I think that's a big problem, that people have just given up. (Group for low income families)

Participants were realistic about the availability of resources, but they still thought it was essential for young people to have secure employment and an economic stake in the country's future:

Well there's not a lot you can do financially because obviously there's only so much that can come out of the Government's reserves, but what you must do for the young, all people, particularly the young, is give them something to live for, a hope for tomorrow, and employment is an absolute must, you've got to allow young people, 16-18, to feel that they've got something to go on for, that they too can get married, that they too can have children, raise children. All right they're not going to be executives but at least say to them we've got something for you to do here, a job, not just a job for a week, but a job perhaps for a few years, longer hopefully. Because to say to those children, or to those young men and young women I should say, there's no hope, there's no future for you, sorry, but you won't work for many years, it's no wonder they turn on society, it's no wonder they turn to drugs. (Group of unemployed people, London)

People also talked about sharing what work there was. Another unemployed person in the same discussion said:

But then everybody do job sharing.

EMPLOYMENT AND TRAINING

It became clear from discussions that participants were cynical about government sponsored employment training schemes and especially about youth schemes operating at the time of the study (before the Labour Government's New Deal Policy). Many called for the urgent reform of such schemes, for example:

> YTS is a right con. Companies actually get paid to take on these kids and these kids are doing a full week's work same as any other man that's there, but they're getting £34.00 or something. (Group for low income families)

A common sentiment was that training allowances should be substantially improved:

> I think that young people today would be motivated as well if they were offered more money on YTS schemes. They're getting the same money on YTS schemes as they're getting on income support so do you want to get up at the same time as your neighbour who's been lain in bed for the same money and been working 40 hours a week on a YTS scheme. (Young people's project)

People also questioned the eligibility criteria of such schemes, for example one talked of the discrimination which many men and short-term unemployed people faced when trying to retrain:

> You've got lots of double standards with things when you're going for different courses and jobs and that, some you can get on but only if you've been unemployed for six months or a year, others if you're a woman. I think men get quite victimised in some ways when they get poverty struck because they're supposed to be stronger and able to cope. (Group of lone parents, Yorkshire)

Some participants thought that employment training schemes were beyond reform. This unemployed person thought that the funding devoted to these schemes would be much better spent creating opportunities for permanent employment or improving existing conditions:

> Decent wages, higher wages. Get rid of these bloody ET and YT schemes because the people that are taking ET and YT schemes on, they need workers, they need the workers but they're just not prepared to pay the money. They ought to get rid of these and have proper government grants because the industries just can't afford to

take them on, they ought to help them, help employed people get owt, them that are self-employed can't get owt, there should be something that the government can help them with. (Group of unemployed people, Yorkshire)

Many people made the link between educational attainment and career success. They thought that cuts in education, especially in economically disadvantaged areas, made finding permanent employment extremely difficult for low academic achievers. They saw investment in education, rather than in employment training which they regarded as 'dead-end', as the priority. For example:

If you left school with something like eleven GCSEs you've got a good chance like of going into further education and getting a job for yourself, but I mean if you left school with nothing now that education's been cut back, the chances of leaving school with a good qualification has gone down hasn't it? So they're like _____, they're _____ up from the start, from the start. (Group of young people)

A MINIMUM WAGE?

Some participants thought that government should introduce a minimum wage (when a minimum wage was not the then government's policy). In one group, people debated whether a minimum wage or wage curbs would be a better way of reducing poverty:

A minimum wage, not a maximum wage like you said, a minimum wage.

I think it comes to the same thing, but anyway, yes.

I would like a maximum wage. I always said, if I could give up my car, because I happen to have a nice car, if I could give it up so that everybody would not have cars, I would, I'd just give the keys straight away. So I'm more in the idea of being equal. I know if you look at China it hasn't always worked has it? Or Russia especially. Because we want to improve and improve, partly humans always want to be better than everyone else so that will disappear, so for humans it doesn't tend to work does it? (LETS group)

SUMMARY

INVOLVING POOR PEOPLE

- Most participants thought that poverty debates and developments should fully involve people with experience of poverty. They felt that this involvement had long been denied poor people;
- They recognised that there were difficulties in involving people in and getting support for both local and national anti-poverty initiatives, related to people's prior experience and lack of confidence; the practical problems of campaigning and the need for funding. At the same time, they thought that the involvement of poor people was essential for effective anti-poverty action;
- They thought that the process of involving people with experience of poverty worked best starting locally and could be developed through networking and information exchange;
- They also emphasised the importance of poor people's representation on decision-making bodies affecting them and the need for policy makers to be accountable for their decisions.

TACKLING POVERTY

Participants offered many other proposals for tackling poverty. These can be grouped under three headings, all of which call for action at government level. They demand changes in:

- General government policy: including greater government commitment to tackling poverty, increased investment and more effective anti-poverty programmes;
- Government social policy: including reform of benefits, housing, child support and child care policies to reduce poverty and increase poor people's access to employment and leisure facilities;
- Government employment policy: including more support for and better job creation, education, training and employment.

Participants, however, did not see it solely as government's responsibility to tackle poverty. They also highlighted:

- the initiatives which they themselves were taking, establishing and running self-help, support, educational and economic initiatives;
- their desire for employment to take them out of poverty;
- the efforts they were making, actively seeking employment.

Part Three

THE WAY FORWARD

INTRODUCTION

At the beginning of this book, we included a quotation from Will Hutton where he referred to the silence of poor people. This was his explanation for it:

> In 1902…the Times thundered that a large proportion of the poor were 'miserable mainly from their own fault' – a reaction not seriously shaken as another Rowntree inquiry 90 years later reports similar findings.
>
> So overwhelming is this view in popular culture that the poor share it; even if they resent their lot, they believe that they have no right to expect any different – and those that do find marginalisation so lowers their self-worth that they become accomplices in their own devaluation.[1]

Our study points to the possibility of something very different. Although clearly popular culture impacts on poor people, as it does others, the people with experience of poverty who took part in this project expressed a widespread feeling that poor people either aren't asked their views or aren't listened to. A similar picture is emerging from other projects which involve poor people.[2] Poor people's exclusion is confused with their acquiescence and reluctance or inability to take part. It is then only a short step to dismiss all poor people as passive and apathetic. But is the problem primarily that poor people don't want to speak, or that others prefer not to listen? It is only by having opportunities and forums to express their views that poor people can make clear what *they* think.

NOTES

1   W Hutton, *Why the Poor Remain Silent, Guardian,* 13 February 1995.
2   H Russell (editor), *Speaking From Experience: Voices at the National Poverty Hearing,* Church Action on Poverty, 1996; UK Coalition Against Poverty, Participation Sub-Group, *Poverty and Participation: Learnings from a September 1996 workshop bringing together people living in poverty throughout the UK,* UK Coalition Against Poverty, 1997.

8 Conclusion

WHY IS THIS RESEARCH DIFFERENT?

When we showed one welfare professional a draft of Part Two of this book he said, 'Very interesting, but where is the analysis?' It is an important question, carrying with it assumptions built up by years of poverty research. The second part of the book *does* offer analysis. It is the analysis of poor people *themselves*; their ideas, interpretations, questions, priorities, beliefs and conclusions. Instead of using 'quotations' to illustrate points made by the researchers, poor people's comments and discussions make up the main body of the text, with our comment limited to introducing and linking them. In the main part of the book, we have tried to avoid imposing any analysis of our own on what participants said, but instead tried to enable them to speak for themselves.

Most discussions about poverty have denied people with direct experience of it a voice. Conventional research into poverty tends to be based on answers from individuals on low incomes to fixed questions pre-set by the researcher. While in more qualitative studies, there may be scope for individuals to respond in depth, the questions still tend to be confined to the effects of poverty. The focus here has gone beyond the *effects* of poverty, so that people in poverty can become actors able to engage in discussions about the meaning and politics of poverty and not simply victims able to talk only about the personal impact of poverty.

In drawing up this research project, we were able to build on what people with experience of poverty said at the 1990 meeting *Working Together Against Poverty*. The key issues raised at that meeting, which centrally included how poor people were presented, how they defined poverty, the causes and effects of poverty and the part that poor people could play in anti-poverty action, were adopted as the major focuses of this research.[1]

The framework for research has usually been set by the researcher, but here we have tried to do something different. This was consistent with our aim which was to enable participants to have *their* say in helping to shape the dominant poverty agenda. Although a research framework was still set, the impetus for it came from the earlier meeting in York. By applying it flexibly, using a semi-structured schedule, we hoped that it would further help poor people to contribute to the debate, to offer their views and ideas about these issues and to influence the future direction of debate.

As originally conceived the project would have involved a number of stages which would have enabled the involvement of poor people in the drawing up of the original research agenda, bringing them together to work out how they wanted to undertake the research, their areas of interest and perhaps carrying out research themselves, but we could not get funding to do this. This reflects a more general difficulty in getting funding for people who are the subjects of policies and problems to undertake their own research and initiatives.[2] However it is an important direction to go in if truly emancipatory and 'user controlled' research is to be undertaken. We hope we may still be able to do this in the future.

This research was different in two other ways. Carrying out the research through group discussion, rather than individual interviews, permitted a less individualistic approach and allowed people to develop their views through exchange and debate. There is more scope for participants to develop the research agenda through such a process of group discussion. As part of our commitment to participation, transcripts were returned to groups for comment and at the stage of initial editing, we sent participants a first draft and gave them the chance to delete or alter any of their comments which we intended to use in the final version.

THEMES AND ISSUES

In this chapter, we pull together some of the themes and issues which emerge, both from the project and from what people with experience of poverty said in it. In doing this, we offer some of our own thoughts and analysis, from our different backgrounds, as well as making links with wider discussions and literature about poverty. We are anxious not to overshadow what people say and we recognise that other interpretations may also be placed upon their comments. We are not trying to impose a 'grand narrative' of our own, but rather to explore some of the connections between what people said in different discussions, in different parts of the country.

We begin by looking at what people with experience of poverty said about the key elements of the dominant poverty discussion.

WHAT IS POVERTY?

Definition has become a central problem in discussions about poverty. This is reflected particularly in what is presented in political and media discussions as the polarisation of opposing absolute and relative definitions of poverty. Although when asked, some participants subscribed to a relative definition, *all* the groups tended towards an absolute definition of poverty. They thought that it was of a different kind and magnitude to poverty experienced in the Third World and that the kind of poverty they associated with the South was 'real' poverty. Interestingly, when talking about poverty generally and talking about their own experience, as opposed to definitions as such, participants tended to see poverty in more relative terms.

Furthermore, when we asked people to define poverty in their own words, their definitions tended to be idiosyncratic and personal. For example, one group thought that having to apologise for owning a lawnmower meant being in poverty. This subjectivity carried over into discussions about whether people were themselves 'poor'. Some thought they were, but most felt they were merely 'hard-up' or 'worse-off' than some other people. Runciman explores the way people experience deprivation in his thesis of relative deprivation.[3] In a way similar to his findings, despite the evidence they gave that they were poor compared to most members of society, many participants experiencing relative deprivation, did not perceive themselves to be 'poor', on the basis that they thought there were others worse off than themselves. This underlines the complexities of the relationship between more 'subjective' and 'objective' definitions and understandings of poverty.

On a casual reading, people's comments might be seen to offer some comfort to the political right, with their support for an absolute definition of poverty and the distinction they drew between UK and Third World poverty. But the contradiction between people's formal definitions and their accounts of their own harsh experience is central to understanding here. People's denial of poverty has previously been explained in terms of their unwillingness to accept the stigma of being poor or needing to see someone in a worse position than themselves to maintain their own self-esteem. But what poor people in this project also communicated strongly, was a reluctance out of *altruism* to couple their own predicament with that of other people, both in the South and the UK, whose situation they felt was much worse than theirs, as if by doing so they would belittle the even harsher circumstances of others.

The common-sense appeal which the absolute definition of poverty carries may also point to the need for a shift from the present preoccupation with poverty lines, which both narrows the issue and results in an over-emphasis on the material conditions of poverty. Readers may recall that some participants offered psychologically and spiritually based, as well as material definitions of poverty. Some also talked about poverty in terms of their rights being restricted. This relates to broader discussion about the way in which poverty excludes people from the full rights of citizenship.[4] Such an approach highlights ways in which poverty limits people's capacity to fulfil their personal and social responsibilities as well as to secure their rights and applies equally to North and South. It is expressed, for example, in Oxfam's Global Charter for Basic Rights, which says:

Everyone has a basic right to:

- a home,
- clean water,
- enough to eat,
- a safe environment,
- protection from violence,
- equality of opportunity,
- a say in their future,
- an education,
- a livelihood,
- healthcare.

It also relates to the increasing interest being shown by some analysts in conceptualising poverty in terms of the social relations of *power*. For example:

> The concept of social exclusion has moved the focus from poverty as a relative condition, resolved through distributional mechanisms, to an understanding of poverty as a *relational* dynamic. In other words, poverty is about more than access to material resources, it is about the social relations of power and control, the processes of marginalisation and exclusion, and the complex and multifaceted ways in which these operate.[5]

There continues to be little agreement about the definition of poverty. What we can say, is that the rather simplistic nature of the absolute/relative poverty dichotomy is illuminated further when poor people themselves have their say.

IMAGES OF POVERTY

Many people who took part in the project were very critical of the images and ideas about poor people presented by the political and academic right and in the media, particularly the right-wing press. Most felt that politicians and media labelled poor people as dangerous, disaffiliated, deviant and dependent. They saw ideas like the 'underclass', 'dependency', 'scrounging' and welfare 'queue jumping' as lumping together and stigmatising poor people generally. Many participants saw these ideas as having some small basis of truth, but to have been distorted, magnified and taken out of context by politicians and media for their own purposes. Participants were mostly, if not always, understanding, rather than condemning of such behaviour on the part of poor people. Many people felt that Conservative governments were directly or indirectly to blame for people being poor, in situations like their own. So far the election of a Labour government does not seem to have marked any significant shift in either media or politicians' imagery of poverty, with the same emphasis on 'dependency', the 'underclass' and scroungers.

While many people expressed distrust of both politicians and media, their relationship with, and understanding of, the media also seemed complex. Some participants accepted the news cutting about 'professional' begging at face value. Some of those who believed in the existence of an 'underclass', might be included in it themselves but often seemed unaware of this. The dominant imagery of poverty seems to mediate people's own experience as well as the understanding of others. We were left with the feeling that it was difficult to over-estimate the importance of the media in shaping all our understandings of poverty and in shaping poverty agendas.

The approach we used to explore the media's portrayal of poverty and poor people, through press cuttings, had strengths and weaknesses. Participants generally found it accessible and helpful. However, it didn't necessarily address all the issues which it would be helpful to explore with poor people, for example, what does and doesn't get media coverage, the personalising of poverty, and concepts which are currently prominent like 'social exclusion' and 'dependency culture' and these would benefit from further examination.

The stigma and negative identity attached to poor people was a central issue for many participants. They thought that this stigma was carried over into all aspects of people's everyday lives, with others treating them differently and negatively just because they were poor. It was difficult for participants to see how this stigma could be overcome. They also talked at some length about the terms that are used in conventional discussions, like 'poor' and 'poverty'. Most thought that these terms were negative and potentially stigmatising. Few, however, could come up with alternatives. A helpful area for future enquiry would be to consider the language of poverty in the broader context of language, power and inequality.

WHAT CAUSES POVERTY?

Despite the limited opportunities many participants had previously had to develop their analysis or take part in discussions about poverty, they had very clear views as to poverty's causes. Most thought that it was caused by a combination of many different social processes. They generally located the causes of poverty in the *social structure*, not in the individual. The structural explanations which they put forward can be grouped into four sets of causes:

- Politico-economic: which derive from the adverse effects of the market economy, with most emphasis on unemployment;
- general government policy: especially in relation to wage differentials and privatisation;
- government social security policy: in particular inadequate benefit levels;
- more general social policies and issues: notably housing and discrimination.

Although only a few participants saw the causes of poverty as lying within the individual, this did not seem to reflect any attempt to off-load responsibility. Many people also talked at length about the efforts which they and other poor people they knew made to challenge the structural constraints which they faced and improve their situation. Their inability to do so is a measure of the strength of these constraints. This combination of agency and structure in their accounts is reflected in some of the more recent academic writing on poverty.[6]

WHAT ARE THE EFFECTS OF POVERTY?

It is perhaps not surprising that poor people taking part in the discussions saw the effects of poverty as overwhelmingly negative and affecting people in many different and subtle ways at the same time. These effects were also pervasive, affecting every aspect of people's lives.

They thought poverty affected people psychologically, leading to loss of self-esteem, anger, depression, anxiety and boredom. Participants placed a greater emphasis on such psychological effects of poverty than conventional poverty discussions usually do. They also highlighted its physical effects, leading to ill-health. Many spoke of its damaging effects on personal relationships and the way it stigmatised people. People also talked about a wide range of practical ill-effects poverty had, restricting people's opportunities and choices, limiting what they can and can't do, where they can and can't be and making budgeting a never-ending tyranny. Poverty not only stopped people doing things for themselves. It also prevented them from contributing to the wider society as they wanted to – an aspect of being poor which has figured less often in conventional research findings. There were also some interesting omissions in what people said. While, for example, they talked about poverty causing crime, they did not discuss poor people as victims of crime. One group, however, did raise with the worker their concerns about the general level of violence in society.

Many people felt *trapped* in poverty; excluded from the labour market or restricted to low paid and part-time jobs and forced to rely on benefits. They felt they were kept in a position of 'dependence', rather than opting for it themselves and that this was not caused primarily by the nature of welfare, but by the nature of the labour market and the economy

A few people also identified positive effects of poverty. Some believed that one way to cope was to 'accentuate the positive' by

looking on poverty as a challenge and trying to turn it into a kind of
game which they could win by surviving and living their lives as best
they could.

THE EFFECTS ON CHILDREN

Participants placed particular emphasis on the destructive effects
which poverty had on children and young people. This reinforces the
findings of conventional research. The effects on children and young
people were a cause of concern for all groups – older people, parents
and young people themselves – and this was raised in many parts of
the discussions. Poor people identified a number of alarming problems:

- the deprivation of children;
- the damaging effects of poverty on relationships between children
  and parents because of the stress and hardship it created;
- the particular poverty facing 16-18-year-olds caused by benefit
  restrictions;
- increasing conflicts between parents and young people caused by
  social policy reforms, for example, in housing and welfare benefits;
- the lack of prospects for today's young people;
- fears for the future arising from fears that the situation is getting
  worse.

Parents, particularly mothers and lone parents, spoke of the enormous
sacrifices they made for their children and expressed real fears about
'what there will be for them' in the future.

HOW TO TACKLE POVERTY?

Most participants felt that people with experience of poverty should
play a central role in anti-poverty action. Many said they were willing
to be involved in both local and national initiatives, but saw local
activities as the starting point. People recognised that there were
difficulties attached to campaigning, not least overcoming people's
lack of confidence and experience and securing funding. Some had
personal experience of these problems. Involvement meant different
things to different people. Some saw it in terms of poor people being
represented on decision-making bodies; others believed that it meant
making policy-makers accountable to policy users. Some saw self-
help initiatives like LETS and food co-ops as a way of getting
involved and others talked about campaigns, self-organisation and
direct action. Again there was recognition that initiatives directly

involving poor people would need support from and links with professionals already involved in anti-poverty and related work. Some participants already had such positive relations. There was also a feeling that if poor people made the effort to become involved, then politicians and policy makers should also take the initiative and come and speak with 'people like us', and listen to what they said.

Most participants thought that government had a crucial role to play in tackling poverty. This extended to a much greater commitment in general policy to reduce poverty; through reform of social policy, including benefits, housing, child support and child care policies; and in employment policy, with a much greater commitment to and investment in job creation, education and training.

REFLECTIONS ON THE PROJECT

There is much that is new and interesting in what poor people had to say in this project; much of it has also been said before. In many ways it is similar to what researchers and pressure groups have been saying for a long time. This does not reduce its significance. What is important and different is that this is what some people with experience of poverty *themselves* think. It cannot be dismissed as the arguments of lobbyists or 'experts' with an axe to grind. Here poor people speak for themselves. This study begins to reveal their own conceptualisation, interpretations and priorities. Participants were not offering their responses to narrow preset questions, like, for example: 'Would you like to see change in government benefits policy?', but able to offer more flexible responses to broader areas of enquiry and express their own independent thoughts and proposals. When they said that poverty equalled powerlessness, it was *they* rather than researchers who were making the connection. Instead of being provided with the categories, they came up with their own. The similarities between what they said and findings from conventional research, which it often confirms, should not hide the fact that these are poor people's *own* views, not their responses to those of other people. It is an important distinction which points to a different way of discussing and campaigning against poverty.

BUT ARE THEY 'REPRESENTATIVE'?

A wide range of people with experience of poverty took part in the project, but there is still the question of how 'representative' or 'typical' they and their views are of poor people more generally. One criticism which we expect to encounter is that they were not typical of people with experience of poverty because they were 'activists'. It is true, as we have said, that some participants had been involved in campaigning and anti-poverty initiatives. Most had some kind of affiliation and this was the way in which we were able to make contact with them. But there was a wide range of such affiliations and most were not based on campaigning or being heavily involved in social action. Some of the groups were family support groups; some were women's groups; some were age related groups, like the groups for older people and for young homeless people; some were support groups for claimants and some were community and self-help groups. Only a minority of these groups were also involved in social action. Some people were 'politicised', many more were not. We worked hard to include poor people beyond the networks of those already actively involved in anti-poverty action, although this is one of the real difficulties facing anti-poverty initiatives which aim to be participatory.

One thing which the project underlines is that there is no such thing as a 'typical' poor person. It is important to challenge stereotypes. Participants in our project ranged from people who could not read or write, to university graduates. More and more people are now exposed to poverty and being poor affects people in different ways. We are only likely to know how representative of poor people participants were when more poor people have their chance to have a say.

The discussion about the 'representativeness' of marginalised groups has already been well rehearsed in debates about 'user involvement' in community care, where disabled people, people with learning difficulties, mental health service users and other groups routinely encounter the criticism that they are 'unrepresentative'. The response of these groups is that this argument is generally raised because they challenge the status quo or do not conform with stereotypes of them as passive, inarticulate and incompetent. Because they have routinely been excluded, the very act of being involved and the people who become involved are assumed to be unusual and atypical. Their response is to argue for support for more people to become involved, to ensure the inclusion of the widest possible range of views.[7]

THE SAME BUT DIFFERENT?

There were many shared feelings and experiences among the poor people who took part in this project; across different groups and in different parts of the country. But there were also important differences. We certainly are not suggesting that there is one view about poverty among poor people. Instead a much richer and more complicated picture begins to emerge. People disagreed and argued in the same group. Groups faced different problems and poverty affects people in different ways. Different groups sometimes had specific concerns and priorities; for example, unemployed people about unemployment. Individuals who had been involved in anti-poverty action seemed to find it easier to talk in structural terms; while those who hadn't were more likely to develop proposals for action from personal experience. Both, however, were critical of Conservative administrations.

It is also possible to detect some differences between participants according to age, gender and to some extent 'race'. For example, young people tended to be more critical of party politics, suspicious of institutions and distrustful of politicians and the political process as a means of positive change. Older people were just as critical, but their arguments were grounded in experience, often comparing the past with the present and expressing bitterness about what they saw as the disintegration of the welfare state and cradle to grave health, welfare, education and pensions. Differences between men and women were most pronounced when discussing the causes and effects of poverty. Men tended to talk in more macro/societal terms about the class structure, mass redundancy and economic recession; women talked more in micro/household terms about low levels of benefits creating budgeting and child care problems. Women placed particular emphasis on the effects of poverty on the individual, family, relationships and children. This reflects women's role as managers of poverty within families.[8] Because of the relatively small number of Black and minority ethnic participants, it is difficult to draw firm conclusions from what they said, but there did seem to be a slight tendency for them to talk more about structural discrimination and stigma in all its expressions.

The operation of social divisions among poor people was also reflected in discriminatory comments made by a small number of participants. There were some racist and sexist comments and criticisms of beggars and homeless people. Some non-disabled people criticised disabled people because of the higher benefits they received, without taking into account the additional expenses they incurred and there were some attacks on lone parents from young men and older people.

LESSONS TO BE LEARNED FROM THE PROJECT

As well as enabling people with experience of poverty to make their contribution to the poverty debate, the research also highlights a number of particular issues about poor people and poverty discussion.

- The project offers further confirmation that people with experience of poverty are able to take part in debates about poverty and have a valuable contribution to make. We sought to engage with poor people as subjects. Participants clearly valued the idea of having what they say reported as they said it; standing in its own right and not just interpreted by 'experts'.
- People were keen to participate and to have a voice. It was a common theme across groups. It was not only people with experience in campaigns and groups who expressed this view. It extended across discussion groups, including, for example, the group of young ex-offenders and of older people. It was reflected both in their interest in the discussion and their more general desire to 'have a say.' While it may be argued that these groups were to some extent self-selecting, their participation refutes the argument that it is difficult or impossible to involve poor people.
- Participants in the project challenged the conventional presentation of poor people as either sad or bad. Whether they were talking about their own experience or broader issues, they communicated a strong sense of openness and honesty and a distinct lack of self-pity. Despite the often appalling difficulties and constraints which they faced, an underlying attitude was one of 'making the best of it', a willingness to change their circumstances and an interest in self-improvement.
- Poverty is an isolating experience. The claimant's role is now highly individualised. Employment and welfare policies have, until very recently, increasingly discouraged people from taking part in voluntary action, adult learning and other activities which would offer opportunities to get together with others. Not only did individuals who took part in the project often feel isolated, so did groups. Participants repeatedly said that they would like to make

contact with others involved in similar activities and we tried to support such networking by putting people who wanted it in touch with each other and interested organisations.

- Poor people do not necessarily accept the terms of the dominant political debate about poverty. While, for example, some people taking part in the project shared left-of-centre views, talking about the need for more state intervention or redistribution, they generally did not adopt traditional old left/right positions or New Labour ones. This was also true for people with political affiliations. First hand knowledge of the realities of poverty seemed to discourage most people from accepting conventional ideological positions.

- So far people with experience of poverty have had few chances to develop their own discussion. While new initiatives are now emerging, poor people have so far received little support to take part in poverty debates and developments. Such support is needed for people to gain the confidence, information and experience to take part fully and effectively. This is also the lesson of the experience of related movements, like the disabled people's movement. Some participants in the project, for example, found it very difficult to answer more open and abstract questions, particularly about the definition of poverty and proposals for the future, although we tried to present them clearly and carefully. This seemed to be because they hadn't previously had the opportunities to explore them, or the information with which to do so.

- Nevertheless, people with experience of poverty have their own views and ideas on the subject. They do not just reflect dominant values and attitudes and are not only influenced by them. The argument that they have nothing new or additional to offer because of their internalisation of ruling values or their inability to express their own views, does not hold. Some of the people involved in our project also had contact with anti-poverty, voluntary and other campaigning organisations and were also familiar with their ideas, language and aspirations and sometimes shared them.

- There may be problems around people organising on the basis of being poor, because of the stigma associated with it. But this project also suggests that organising solely on the basis of the particular identities associated with poverty, for example, being a lone parent, disabled, young or old, may create other problems by reinforcing divisions between groups. The reluctance of some people to be identified with poverty is not an argument for excluding people with experience of poverty or for not supporting their involvement in anti-poverty initiatives. Instead it may have broader implications for how existing debates and campaigns organise and address the issues associated with poverty if they are to be more inclusive.

A BASIS FOR INVOLVEMENT

The methodology which we used in the Poverty First Hand project, while encountering some difficulties and problems (see Appendix One) does give promise for the future. Although the research schedule set the context for the discussions, we made every effort to ensure that participants could raise their own thoughts and ideas. Moreover, the discussions appeared to allow people a space in which to share and rehearse these thoughts and ideas with others, giving poor people a chance to learn from each other's experience. In these circumstances people seemed willing to talk frankly with others about issues close to them. These discussions give encouragement for the successful involvement of more people in the future.

As we have indicated, the views of people with experience of poverty seemed to be consistent with and to complement many of those that have been put forward in conventional discussions about poverty by 'experts', including academics, politicians and anti-poverty organisations. As some participants acknowledged, discussions involving and drawing on the knowledge of poor people cannot exist in isolation from conventional poverty debate. The voice of poor people needs to be developed with the support of these other constituencies if it is to be effective.

The discussions demonstrate that while poor people are not all the same, they do share a number of key common concerns which provide a basis for collective action. Most participants, far from being apathetic or defeated, made it clear that they were willing to participate in future anti-poverty initiatives, despite the known difficulties, both locally and nationally. This is not to suggest that all poor people want to take part in anti-poverty action. What is clear, however, is that an interest in involvement and change does exist.

PROPOSALS FOR THE FUTURE

Although participants in the project had many proposals to make, we don't think it is appropriate for us to offer a set of recommendations for future anti-poverty action. The aim of this project was to open up the debate about poor people's involvement, rather than trying to provide a detailed blueprint for action. We see it as just one stage in a long term project for the participation of poor people. This book points to the need for a changed *process* in anti-poverty debate and policy, which involves poor people, rather than offering a prescription for their content or direction. It demonstrates that the issue is not whether poor people share the same view, but that their different views should be included in the debate. This relates to a similar distinction drawn in some feminist writing between a group's shared *interests* – in being involved and represented – and a group's *concerns*, which will not necessarily be unified.[9]

We know that poor people who took part in the project valued being involved, wanted to be able to network with others with experience of poverty, wanted more opportunities to be involved themselves and for poor people more generally to be involved. Other work is beginning to present a similar picture.[10] Thus the goal must be to find ways of enabling the full and effective involvement of people with experience of poverty. With the election of a government promising a 'new politics', the potential is there to transform and revitalise the politics of poverty through the involvement of people with experience of poverty.

However a number of difficulties remain. It was not possible in this project, despite strenuous efforts, to involve all the constituencies of poor people that we wished to, including, for example, travellers, people in low paid employment, young people leaving care, refugees and Black groups. We know that other initiatives seeking to involve people with experience of poverty have experienced similar problems in opening up and increasing poor people's involvement. This problem is both an expression of and a continuing obstacle in the way of challenging the exclusion of poor people. All these groups must be reached if the multiplicity of voices of people in poverty is to be heard. For these voices to develop further and bring positive change, they need to be able to engage with conventional discussions of poverty. Poor people must have the opportunity to debate the issues and ideas that concern them, both among themselves and in safe settings with academics, politicians, the media and anti-poverty professionals. The Poverty First Hand project, together with the earlier meeting in York which inspired it, is one step in bringing people together to talk about these issues. There are now also others. We hope that they will inspire further steps.

People with experience of poverty are still marginalised in poverty debate. Much has still to be accomplished before they become central to anti-poverty action. In this book, participants have stressed the need for poor people to have their own voice at national and local levels. The goal must be to find ways of enabling the full and effective involvement of people with experience of poverty. The lesson from other areas of policy is that for this to happen, a coherent programme of action will be needed.[11] Key elements of this include:

- ensuring that all key stakeholders are involved;
- developing ways of enabling poor people's full involvement;
- identifying obstacles to poor people's participation and ways of overcoming them.

There are a number of specific initiatives which may help make this possible. These include:

- Providing forums, opportunities, support and space for people with experience of poverty to come together and develop their own discussion to put alongside those of academics, traditional pressure groups, politicians and media;
- Existing anti-poverty organisations, including local authorities with anti-poverty strategies, helping to access and disseminate poor people's own discussion through their own networks and channels of communication;
- Further work to involve and address the specific perspectives of particular groups with experience of poverty, particularly women, Black people and members of minority ethnic groups, young and older people, lesbians and gay men and disabled people;
- Further adequately-funded participatory research to explore and develop the perspectives of people with experience of poverty, particularly research by and under the control of people with experience of poverty themselves;
- The funding of umbrella organisations controlled by people with experience of poverty and employment of people with experience of poverty as workers, in order to link poor people and their local organisations and enable them to share information about local activities, groups and initiatives to help to develop more

broadbased, inclusive and effective anti-poverty action;

- A review of the processes and goals of anti-poverty organisations to facilitate the increased involvement of people with experience of poverty; many poor people do not seem to have signed up to the prevailing anti-poverty analysis. It is difficult to see how there can be effective pressure for change when the people directly affected by poverty and most at risk of it, deny its existence or do not share the interpretations which are being offered;
- An urgent public debate involving poor people about the role of the media in the presentation of poverty, as a basis for developing guidelines and an effective code of practice, to ensure that the media deal responsibly and fairly with poor people in the future.

POVERTY: A PROBLEM FOR ALL OF US

For us the importance of involving poor people in poverty debates and the need to do this in a participatory way, are summed up by this exchange between the project's first worker and members of the women's education group, who took part in the project, towards the end of their discussion. It highlights the value both of shared experience and a more equal research relationship. This enables the subjects of research to ask their own questions, think through their own issues and develop their own knowledge. Where the researcher also has experience of poverty, s/he is able to draw on it to respond to them.

Can I ask you a question, now you're sitting there?

Yes sure.

What do you think, you look around us, do you think any of us are poor?

As you said, you know you can only relate to what you know. I can only relate to poverty as when I knew it when I was small and it was kind of strange because when I was small we were very poor. To me it was actually great because we had no money because my mother's step-mother died and so we had to have her half-brothers and sisters come and live with us, so there were 10 of us in three bedroom house and we all had to share beds and stuff. But to me I can only remember it as being really great because I had lots of people around.

Did you know you were poor?

Yes I knew we were poor one day because I remember I came home and I had like holes in my shoes and it was raining and my feet were wet and I said like 'I need some new plimsolls for school' and my mum said 'you can't have any because we don't have any money' so she painted some cardboard black and put them in the bottom of my plimsolls. And I suppose I was probably about seven or eight...

And do you consider today you've been talking to poor people or not? Where would you categorise us? You've asked us what we think poverty is, what do you think?

It's difficult because some of you were saying that you don't consider yourselves poor ... If you want the gospel truth, I would say that to me, I think most of you are poor, and that's my honest answer, that's what I honestly think.

I'm damned poor.

I'm poor.

When we were trying to make contact with people with experience of poverty to take part in the project, we sent out many letters, leaflets and flyers. One woman got in touch who said that she was not 'materially' affected by poverty, but nonetheless felt she was 'adversely affected by it'. She said:

Poverty worries me. It keys me up ... I argue with my friends and colleagues, I overwork and become stressed and exhausted, frustrated and wonder if I or the world is insane, continually feeling as if on the brink of a great pit, attempting to hold on, knowing I will not fall into poverty myself, but into a pit of despair where I will be unable to do even the little I do now. These feelings are brought on by working with children who are needing more to eat, more physical exercise, more space, more adult attention ... They are also brought on by walking down the high street which is filled with charity shops, young people selling the Big Issue, young people begging, older people who are clearly unwell.

Poverty affects all of us. It degrades all our lives. All of us have something to say about it. All of us have a part to play in its solution. By ensuring the inclusion of people with experience of poverty, it may at last be possible to put an end to the 'them' and 'us' of poverty.

NOTES

1 R Lister and P Beresford, *Working Together Against Poverty: Involving poor people in action against poverty,* Open Services Project and Department of applied Social Studies, University of Bradford, 1991.

2 C Barnes and G Thompson, *Funding for User-led Initiatives,* British Council of Organisations of Disabled People and National Council for Voluntary Organisations, 1994.

3 W G Runciman, *Relative Deprivation and Social Justice: A study of attitudes to social inequality in twentieth century England,* Penguin, 1966.

4 R Lister, *The Exclusive Society, Citizenship and the Poor,* Child Poverty Action Group, 1990.

5 F Williams with J Pillinger, *New Thinking an Social Policy Research into Inequality, Social Exclusion and Poverty,* in J Millar and J Bradshaw (editors), Social Welfare Systems: Towards a Research Agenda, University of Bath/ESRC, 1996.

6 see, for example, note 5 above and R Lister, *In Search of the 'Underclass',* Introduction to Charles Murray and the Underclass Debate, IEA Health and Welfare Unit, 1996.

7 P Beresford and J Campbell, *Disabled People, Services Users, User Involvement and Representation,* Disability and Society, Volume 9, No 3, 1994, pp315-325.

8 R Lister, *Women in Poverty,* in K Funken and P Cooper (editors), Old and New Poverty: The challenge for reform, Rivers Oram Press, 1995.

9 C Cockburn, *Strategies for Gender Democracy: Strengthening the representation of trade union women in the European social dialogue,* European Journal of Woman's Studies, Volume 3 (1), February, 1996, pp7-26.

10 For example, UK Coalition Against Poverty, Participation Sub-Group, *Poverty and Participation: Learnings from a September 1996 workshop bringing together people living in poverty throughout the UK,* UK Coalition Against Poverty, 1997.

11 P Beresford and S Croft, *Citizen Involvement: A practical guide for change,* Macmillan, 1993.

APPENDIX ONE

HOW WE UNDERTOOK THE PROJECT

In many ways this was a pilot project, carried out with limited funds in a limited time and part of its purpose was to test the methodology and methods which we used. We hope that we can adapt these methods to carry out future research involving many more people with experience of poverty and enabling them to play an even fuller part in developing the research.

WHY WE USED A PARTICIPATORY METHODOLOGY

This research used a *participatory* research methodology.[1] We drew on both participatory and emancipatory research approaches. These approaches are linked with what Reason and Rowan called 'new paradigm research, a cluster of approaches including action–research and feminist research[2]. This family of approaches addresses issues which were particularly relevant to us in this project, including the question of objectivity, the validity of subjective insight, the involvement of research subjects in the research process, informed consent in the giving of information, the relationship of research to making change and improving people's lives and the subjectivity of the researcher.[3] As Oakley has argued from a feminist perspective:

> ...the mythology of 'hygienic' research with its accompanying mystification of the researcher and the researched as objective instruments of data production (must) be replaced by the recognition that the personal involvement is more than dangerous bias – it is the condition under which people come to know each other and to admit others to their lives.[4]

The concerns of emancipatory research closely overlap those of participatory research. Emancipatory research is particularly associated with the disabled people's movement. Oliver argues for a different social process for the production of research. He says that disabled people's disillusion with existing disability research led them to develop:

> ...an alternative, emancipatory approach in order to make disability research both more relevant to the lives of disabled people and more influential in improving their material circumstances. The two key fundamentals on which such an approach must be based are

empowerment and reciprocity. These fundamentals can be built in by encouraging self-reflection and a deeper understanding of the research situation by the research subjects themselves as well as enabling researchers to identify with their research subjects.[5]

Key elements of participatory and emancipatory research methodology and methods include:

- people who are the subjects of research having a say in its focus and design;
- undertaking research which accesses and provides opportunities for the development of the perspectives and views of subjects of policy and provision themselves, as well as those of policy makers and providers;
- the involvement of service users themselves as researchers;
- research participants having the right to check, change and withdraw information which they have given;
- feeding back research findings to research participants and their broader constituencies in accessible and appropriate formats.

Although as mentioned in Chapter 8, lack of funds did not permit the direct involvement of people experiencing poverty in the drawing up of the research agenda, it was based on the issues highlighted by participants at the York meeting between people with experience of poverty and anti-poverty professionals.[6] The research sought, as far as possible, to reflect in the analysis and during the editorial process, the thoughts and concerns of participants during the actual discussions themselves. Participation during the group discussions was embodied by the use of a semi-structured schedule and by an attempt to include the views of *all* the participants present without any one individual or sub-group dominating the discussion. The project worker sought to achieve this by a process of sensitive intervention and prompting. On the other hand the project worker also aimed to be non-interventionist in order to allow the discussions to flow as naturally as possible and to allow the research to reflect the agendas of participants as much as it could. The balance between the project workers' intervention and non-intervention was therefore crucial in the facilitation of group discussions.

The analysis of the material from the group discussions used a process of *grounded theory*.[7] Most conventional research tends to try to fit the answers respondents give to questions into pre-determined categories for purposes of analysis. We believed that the views and ideas of participants in the project were the most important ones in this project and not our own. Therefore it was the views and thoughts of participants which were the basis for categorisation, not vice versa. Any theories which were developed were 'grounded' in the ideas and thoughts of participants, rather than in any preconceived ideas which we might have had. Instead of imposing a theoretical framework on what people said, we aimed to let them generate their own theoretical framework.

Participants received a copy of the transcription of their discussion for modification and agreement. They were also given the opportunity of involvement in the initial editing of the book. We sent them a first draft and asked if they wanted to delete or change any of their comments which we intended to use in the final version.

WHY GROUP DISCUSSIONS?

We carried out this project using group discussions for a number of reasons. Conventional poverty research has concentrated on asking individuals questions, usually confined to their own personal experience. One of the messages which comes from what participants say in this book is the way in which poor people are frequently singled out either as individual passive victims or in individualistic critiques as personally responsible for being poor. We used group discussions to try and overcome this individualistic focus, aiming to enable participants' views to develop through interchange and understanding in a 'safe' environment. All group discussions were taped and transcribed so that people's comments could be reproduced as faithfully as possible in this book and so that participants would have a record of their discussion to check and for their information.

WHY WE SPOKE TO THE PEOPLE WE DID

As we have seen, politicians and the media simultaneously appear to lump poor people together as if they were the same as each other and different to other people, while singling out some groups, like single mothers and people claiming benefits, for special criticism. We therefore attempted to do two things:

- include as many different groups as possible to get a broad spectrum of opinion and reflect the diversity of people in poverty;
- include as many of those groups as possible which encounter particular criticism and stigma from the media and politicians.

To get the groups together, we used a process of snowball sampling;[8] that is making contact with large organisations involved in anti-poverty work and through them gaining access to smaller, often local organisations with links to people with experience of poverty. We began by making contact with some of the participants at the York meeting and also drew on our own extensive contacts and networks. As well as approaching groups and organisations working in the poverty field, we also contacted organisations controlled by and for groups at high risk of poverty, like for example, disabled people and older people.

Overall more women than men took part in the project, both in specific women's groups and in mixed groups. This reflects the extent to which women are especially vulnerable to poverty. Older people were represented in both a specific discussion and as members of other groups. There were discussions with groups of young people and disabled people. The project did not include a specific group of Black people or members of minority ethnic groups, but both were included in other groups.

We were also had to address a more fundamental methodological issue in the project. While we cannot be sure that all participants had experienced poverty as it is conventionally defined, we are confident that the vast majority had. But we realised early on that we might be faced with a paradox. How would we select people with direct experience of poverty to take part in the project if our aim was to enable poor people to offer their own views and definitions of poverty and not preempt them? We sought to deal with this by not taking the concept of 'poverty' as given in the literature about the project which we circulated; by making it clear that we recognised that many people did not like the term 'poverty' or necessarily define their experience or conceive of their issues in these terms and by using alternative words. In the information which we sent to groups, we wrote, for example:

> Poverty is in the news. Politicians and the media are saying what they think about the problem and the people who are experiencing it. But this raises a number of problems. Some people who are seen as poor don't like being called poor. They don't see their problems or situation in those terms. They don't think that poverty is necessarily a helpful idea. There isn't agreement about what poverty means. Especially important, people on low income and groups particularly affected by poverty have generally had little chance so far to say what they think

about the subject. The aim of this project is to change this by providing a chance for people with first hand experience of the issues associated with poverty to tell their side of the story.

In this way we hoped we would enable people to define themselves. It is clear from what they said, that while many who took part did not include themselves as poor in one sense, they did in another. The experience, low income and hardship which they reported certainly indicated poverty as we would understand it.

HOW 'REPRESENTATIVE' WERE PARTICIPANTS?

The issue of 'representativeness' has increasingly been raised as oppressed groups have demanded to speak for themselves, or their voices have been prioritised in research. Concerns are frequently expressed by critics of such approaches that the views of people who get involved are atypical and unrepresentative. It is also suggested that people who are actively involved or who take part in campaigning have different views to those who do not. One study of women who were consulted about local government services offers some helpful insights. It revealed that:

> All women shared a remarkable agreement on a wide range of issues. Feminists and non-feminists in particular agreed on a wide variety of practical issues for women, covering every aspect of women's lives, from access to education and facilities for children.
>
> ... it was not possible for management to hide behind the belief that it is only a small number of feminist or middle class women who want changes in the way council services operate.

One difference that did emerge, however, was that:

> Feminists were more likely to express their ideas about council services as demands. In all, a striking feature of the consultation process was the lack of demands. Women could identify a lack of a service but this in the majority of groups did not translate into a demand for action.[9]

Thus women who were more actively involved might not so much have different views as be more effective in achieving them. We are only likely to get a clearer picture as more support is provided for research which enables more people with experience of poverty to speak for themselves.[10] As we mentioned in the last chapter, one tendency which we identified in our research was that groups which were actively involved in anti-poverty action focused more on structural issues and approaches; while those which were not, framed their ideas more in terms of their own experience and interests. But both were critical of the existing government.

RESEARCH ETHICS

Ethics were central to our concerns as researchers.[11] Many of the issues discussed by the participants were sensitive and highly personal. Because of this participants remain anonymous in the book. Unless the groups who took part specifically wished to be identified, their name and exact location is also withheld. There are also broader ethical issues which we have sought to address both by our use of a participatory research methodology and through our focus on the inclusion of people with experience of poverty, like for example, the right of people with experience of poverty to offer their analysis and 'their side of the story'; to tell their whole truth and not just those parts of it that other people might judge acceptable or politic.[12]

THE RESEARCH PROCESS

The research process was quite complex and needs some explanation. The process was as follows:

- Organisations or groups were contacted by telephone and asked if they would like to participate in the project;
- Interested groups and organisations were sent information (see following) about the project by post and then received a follow-up call from the project worker asking if there was any further information they would like or questions they would like to ask. We relied on the contact person to check with people if they wanted to participate in a group discussion. If this was agreed, we would then agree a time and date for the discussion to take place;
- The group discussions lasted for 90 minutes on average, although some were longer. A few did not cover all the areas covered in the semi-structured schedule because of time constraints. Afterwards, a letter thanking people for participating, was sent to groups;
- The discussion was then transcribed and a copy of the transcript sent to the group for correction, modification and agreement. Groups were also asked at this point if they wished to be identified or whether they wanted to remain anonymous in the final version of the book;

- Groups were also offered the opportunity of involvement in the initial editing of the book. We sent them a first draft and asked them if they wanted to delete or change any of their comments which we intended to use in the final version. Sixteen of the groups responded and two made changes which were then incorporated in the final draft.

THE DIFFICULTIES WE ENCOUNTERED

The project encountered a number of difficulties. These problems included:

• ACCESSING GROUPS TO TAKE PART IN THE PROJECT

This was a major problem. Twenty groups took part in the project, but to reach these, we estimate that we contacted at least 250 organisations and groups. This was both time-consuming and demanding. It was because of this problem that we were unable to include some groups which we knew experienced poverty or were at particularly high risk of it. As noted already, we failed to include, for example, people in low paid employment, travellers, students, young people in or who had left care, people with addiction problems and black and minority ethnic organisations. There were a number of reasons for this including: time limits placed on the project; the lack of necessary funds to get such a group together; groups' own fragile situations and competing pressures; or in the case of travellers, because it was difficult to establish and maintain contact with them and they had few opportunities to take part in a discussion. Such difficulties were exacerbated by the isolation which both individual poor people and their organisations frequently experience.

There were also problems because of the very limited involvement of poor people in many anti-poverty organisations and the nature of the relationship between some professionals and poor people. We found that many anti-poverty organisations had very limited contacts or links with poor people. They might, for example, be in touch with a few poor people who would be prepared to talk to the media for them, but they were often wary of risking their own relationship with these poor people. We also encountered one anti-poverty commentator who seemed reluctant to let anyone else have contact with 'their' poor people. A more common problem was anti-poverty

professionals who seemed jealous and over-protective of the poor
people they worked with and acted as gatekeepers, controlling their
outside contacts, deciding *themselves* whether or not they would be
'good for' the group. Some also said, 'We don't want to talk about it.
It's not what we do. Poverty is not an issue for our group', because
they saw the issue in terms of homelessness or low pay rather than
poverty, when by conventional definitions it would appear to have
been an issue. In a number of such cases it was clear that the paid
worker had decided against poor people's participation rather than
enabling poor people to decide for themselves.

• ENSURING PEOPLE'S INFORMED CONSENT

As part of our commitment to a participatory approach to research,
we provided full and accessible information about the project for
potential participants so they would know clearly what it was about,
and be able to make an informed decision about whether they wanted
to take part. This included information about the aims and objectives
of the project, how we were carrying it out, the terms under which
we were seeking people's involvement and the subject areas we
particularly wished to discuss with them. We found that this
information did not always reach them. Where paid workers agreed
to the involvement of groups, it was apparent that frequently they did
not, as agreed, pass information on to people, making comments like
'I forgot' or 'We didn't have time'.

In one case when the project worker met the group, she found
that the worker had not even told them she was coming and she had
to explain the aims of the project and check that people were happy
to take part. After initial difficulties, we provided guidance for
professionals, setting out the principles of the project and how they
might help, for example, by not being present at discussions, unless
participants specifically asked them to be. It was clear, however, that
there were difficulties with workers who were not used to working in
a participatory way. This was in contrast to organisations which
participants controlled themselves, like the organisation of disabled
people, which provided full information inviting people to take part
in the discussion.

We believe that difficulties like those we encountered also reflect
more generally the very limited number of initiatives which there are
so far, either controlled by people with experience of poverty or
involving them fully.

• ENSURING EQUAL INVOLVEMENT

There was sometimes a tension for the project worker between ensuring that everyone has a chance to speak – not only those with a lot to say – and being directive; intervening and interrupting the flow. Getting this balance right proved to be difficult, especially initially, but it became easier as the project workers gained in confidence and skill. Such group facilitation requires considerable sensitivity and skill. To offer support, the first project worker was accompanied by an experienced facilitator at an early discussion and the second project worker was given detailed guidance notes. Both also received regular debriefing and support sessions to check progress and problems.

We also used a series of ground rules, which have been widely used, as a basis for agreement to ensure group discussions were safe, comfortable and positive for participants.[13] These included ground rules about smoking, not interrupting people, confidentiality, enabling everyone to express their views and being able to take time out from the discussion if people wanted a break.

• THE DISCUSSION SCHEDULE

Some parts of the research schedule worked better than others and some of the questions which seemed reasonable in theory, did not work in practice; for example, we talked earlier about the problems when we asked people about differences in the effects of poverty on different groups. If an individual did not understand a question, we would try and rephrase it for them, ensuring that we kept to the original meaning. Some people found it difficult to discuss the conventional definition of poverty, because it was part of a discussion with which they were unfamiliar. Participants also reported some difficulties with the section of the schedule dealing with political and media images of poverty. These tended to be practical problems of people needing time to read the cuttings, pass them round and then move on to the next. One failing in hindsight is that we did not include any material which reflected traditional left of centre perceptions of poor people. Another was that we didn't refer to different concepts prominent in current poverty discussions, such as social exclusion, to see which people found most helpful. We weren't always able to ask all the questions in the schedule. This wasn't only a matter of participants wanting to talk about other things or restrictions on time. Sometimes it might seem inappropriate and intrusive to do so, perhaps leading people to reveal or discuss things about themselves which they might not want to. Where that was the case, we were guided by the need to respect the rights and needs of research participants, prioritised in a participatory research method.

LESSONS FOR THE FUTURE

Time and money were great enemies of this project. Participatory research requires more of both than conventional approaches. Its commitment to the inclusion of all groups on equal terms has a number of cost implications; including the costs of accessible meeting places and transport; support for people to take part, including travelling expenses, interpretation, child care, personal assistance and respite care; and the provision of accessible information in appropriate formats, including, for example, audio cassette, braille, minority ethnic languages and signed video. Some participatory research projects are now also paying participants for their knowledge and expertise.

Participatory research also takes longer because of the need to feed back to people, fitting in with their time schedules and ensure their continuing involvement. In this project, we needed more time to involve people with experience of poverty in formulating the research schedule; to reach as many groups as possible; more time for discussions, so that they weren't rushed and participants could say all they wanted; and more time to involve people in the editorial process. Some participants said they would have liked more time to read through the draft and make changes.

Future research and action by and involving poor people will need more funding if they are to be successful. Funding authorities and trusts should take account of the additional funding needs, if they wish to support more participatory research and anti-poverty initiatives which fully involve people with experience of poverty. Existing experience in related fields is that 'user-led' research and participatory initiatives are at a disadvantage in securing funding, both because of their greater costs and lower credibility than conventional developments.[14] What is likely to be needed is a shift in the allocation of anti-poverty funding to poverty research and initiatives which involve and are led by people with experience of poverty themselves.

As we review our own research process – while we recognise that it had many limitations – our conclusion is that its commitment to participation and the group discussion method was justified. In addition the research schedule, with a few minor alterations, appeared to work and generally reflected the central concerns participants had about poverty. Many of the practical problems encountered in the research could be overcome with more time and resources and could hopefully be ironed out in the planning stage of any future research. We hope it will inspire others to pursue a similar approach.

If the lessons for future research from our project are acted upon, then we are optimistic that the views and proposals of many more people experiencing poverty 'first hand' can be brought into the public arena.

NOTES

1 I Robottom and D Colquhoun, *The Politics of Method in Public Health Research,* in D Colquhoun and A Kellehear (editors), Health Research in Practice: Political, ethical and methodological issues, Chapman and Hall, 1993, p50; W Whyte, *Participatory Action Research,* Sage, 1991, pp20-21.

2 P Reason and J Rowan (editors), *Human Inquiry: A source book of new paradigm research,* John Wiley, 1981.

3 P Beresford, *Researching Citizen Involvement: A collaborative or colonising enterprise?,* in M Barnes and G Wistow, Researching User Involvement, The Nuffield Institute for Health Services Studies, 1992.

4 A Oakley, *Interviewing Women: A contradiction in terms,* in H Roberts (editor), Doing Feminist Research, Routledge, 1982, p58.

5 M Oliver, *Understanding Disability: From theory to practice,* Macmillan, 1996, p141.

6 R Lister and P Beresford, *Working Together Against Poverty: Involving poor people in action against poverty,* Open Services Project and Department of Applied Social Studies, University of Bradford, 1991.

7 B Glaser and A Strauss, *The Discovery of Grounded Theory: Strategies for qualitative research,* Aldine, 1967.

8 G Fennell, *Whom to Study?: Defining the problem,* in S Peace (editor), Researching Social Gerontology, Sage, 1990, p66: P McNeill, *Research Methods,* Tavistock, 1985, p35.

9 H Kettleborough, *Consulting Women in the Community About Local Government Services,* Critical Social Policy, No 12, 1988, pp 56-67.

10 P Beresford and J Campbell, *Disabled People, Service Users, User Involvement and Representation,* Disability and Society, Volume 9, No 3, 1994, pp 315-325.

11 M Bulmer, *Social Research Ethics,* Macmillan, 1982; H Dean (editor), *Ethics and Social Policy Research,* University of Luton Press and Social Policy Association, 1996.

12 P Beresford, *Challenging the 'Them' and 'Us' of Social Policy Research,* in H Dean (editor), Ethics and Social Policy Research, University of Luton

Press and Social Policy Association, 1996.

13 S Croft and P Beresford, *Getting Involved: A practical manual*, Open Services Project, 1993.

14 see note 12.

APPENDIX TWO

THE GROUPS WHICH PARTICIPATED

Twenty groups took part in the project. Some groups were happy to be identified by name, others for various reasons, wished to remain anonymous. Here we provide an, outline of each group, including its location, what it does and a breakdown of participants according to gender, age, 'race' and disability. A total of 137 people took part in the project, of whom 96 were women and 41 men; 122 white and 15 black and members of minority ethnic groups, and 15 disabled.

GROUP OF OLDER PEOPLE

Members of local branches of Age Concern in West London, experiencing problems of poverty. In this area there are large areas of prosperity as well as pockets of extreme deprivation, especially among local minority ethnic groups. The group came together for the launch of a local older people's anti-poverty report.

Six participants all aged over 65; four men of whom three were white and one African-Caribbean and two white women, one Polish.

GROUP OF UNEMPLOYED PEOPLE, LONDON

Members of a centre for unemployed people in Bexleyheath on the outskirts of South-East London.

Six participants, three men and three women, one in his 60s, the rest in their 30s-40s. Five were white and one was of mixed parentage.

WOMEN'S GROUP

Members of a women's group, all of whom were poor, at a Centre in Grimethorpe, a former mining area, now economically depressed. Some of the women had been involved in the Women Against Pit Closures Campaign and anti-poverty initiatives and in campaigns on family issues through the work of the Centre.

Nine women participants, from their 20s – 60s, all of whom were white.

LONE PARENTS GROUP, GLASGOW

All were members of a local branch of One Plus, a national organisation supporting and giving information and advice to lone parent families. 'One Plus is an independent voluntary organisation for lone parents, whether single, widowed, divorced or separated and regardless of sex, sexuality, disability, race, colour or religion. One Plus has a commitment to involve lone parents in its policies and priorities through a community development approach.'

Nine participants, all women, aged between 20 and 45, eight of whom were white, one of whom was Asian.

GROUP OF WOMEN INVOLVED IN CAMPAIGNS

A group of women brought together for the project at the King's Cross Women's Centre, who were involved in different campaigns, including, disability, women's, black and lone parents campaigns

Seven participants, five white and two black, five non-disabled and two disabled, ages ranging from 20s – 60s.

GROUP OF LONE PARENTS, BRISTOL

Single parents who were members of SPAN – the Single Parent Action Network. 'SPAN is a national multi-racial organisation working to improve policies and practice for single parents and children and to support single parent self-help groups in different parts of the country.'

Seven participants, all women, 4 black and three white, ages ranging from 20s to 30s.

MEMBER OF YOUNG PEOPLE'S PROJECT

Users of an accommodation project working with young homeless people in Wakefield, West Yorkshire, which also offers support, advice and counselling. Wakefield has a high level of youth unemployment and a growing rate of homelessness among young people.

Three participants, two young women aged 16 and 17 and one young man, aged 19, all were white.

LETS GROUP

Members of a Local Exchange and Trading System group in Whitstable, on the Kent coast. Such schemes are localised alternatives to a cash economy, where goods and services are exchanged in a non-cash system. Goods produced or services performed are rated on a local LETS currency and each member of the scheme has a LETS account which is credited or debited accordingly. There are more than 300 LETS schemes operating nationally. While some of this area is relatively prosperous, other parts are very deprived. Local coastal towns have high levels of unemployment, especially seasonal unemployment, associated with tourism and agriculture and some have high levels of homelessness.

Five participants, all white, three women and two men, ages ranging from 30s to 70.

WOMEN'S EDUCATION PROJECT

Members of a project for women based in a former coal mining area of West Yorkshire which is specifically concerned with the provision of adult education.

Nine participants, all white women, ages ranging from mid 20s to 50s.

MENTAL HEALTH SERVICE USERS' GROUP

Members of a self-advocacy group in a London borough which has high levels of unemployment and poverty. The group offers advice, support and activities for mental health service users in the area.

Three participants, one white woman, one Asian man and one African-Caribbean man.

GROUP OF YOUNG PEOPLE

Participants were users or ex-users of a residential youth project providing supported and short-term accommodation to young ex-offenders, some on probation; to young people leaving local authority care, and young people judged to be 'at risk'. The project is based in a large affluent town in the south west of England, which also includes some peripheral housing estates and areas of rural poverty.

Seven participants aged between 16 and 20, including five young men and two young women, six white and one African-Caribbean.

GROUP FOR LOW INCOME FAMILIES

Users of an urban centre provided by the local branch of UK voluntary social services organisation in Scotland.

Seven participants, three men and four women, all white.

GROUP OF LONE PARENTS, YORKSHIRE

Members of a local branch of a national organisation for lone parents based in a town in West Yorkshire which has concentrations of urban and local rural poverty.

Nine participants, all women, all white, aged between 20 and 50.

COMMUNITY CENTRE USERS GROUP

Users of a community centre based in a large deprived urban council estate in Scotland.

Seven participants, six women and one man, all white; one teenager, two women aged between 35-45, three aged over 60 and man in his 70s.

RURAL TENANTS GROUP

Members of a tenants association in a rural area of Northumbria with high levels of local unemployment and rural poverty. The association ran a creche, a mother and toddler group and an after-school group for older children, as well as organising leisure and educational activities.

Fifteen participants, eight women and seven men, all white, aged from late teens to 40s.

GROUP OF DISABLED PEOPLE

Members of a local coalition controlled by disabled people, including disabled people from three different groups, based in northern England and linked with similar organisations around the country.

Ten participants, five women and five men, 9 white and one Asian, ages ranging from mid 20s to 60s.

GROUP OF UNEMPLOYED PEOPLE, YORKSHIRE

Users of a centre for unemployed people in a small village in South Yorkshire, with a very high level of local unemployment. The centre provides meals, opportunities for recreation and socialising, training classes, job information and welfare rights advice.

Seven participants, including four women and three men, all white and aged between 25 and 60.

GROUP OF HOMELESS PEOPLE

Users of a project for homeless people situated in London and run by a national organisation campaigning for homeless single people.

Four participants, three men and one women, all white, aged from late 20s to 40s.

ANTI-POVERTY YOUTH GROUP

Members of an anti-poverty youth organisation based in Glasgow, offering support for young unemployed people.

Two white men in their twenties, one disabled and one non-disabled.

WOMEN'S DISCUSSION GROUP

A mixed group of women with direct experience of poverty who came together from different parts of the country for a network news programme on poverty. The group included lone parents, a disabled person, mental health service user and older person.

Five participants, four white and one black and one disabled person.

APPENDIX THREE

THE PROJECT SEMI-STRUCTURED DISCUSSION SCHEDULE

INTRODUCTION

The project worker introduces themselves and offers participants an invitation to ask anything more about them that they like during the course of the discusion.

INTRODUCTORY STATEMENT

I'd like to tell you some more about the project. There is a lot of talk about poverty, disadvantage and deprivation, particularly now. Politicians and the media have a lot to say about it. We don't often hear what people who know about these things first hand have to say. People talk about poverty lines, the number of people in poverty and make assumptions about certain groups being poor.

But there are a lot of problems. People don't agree about what they mean by poverty or being poor. Some people don't think it is a very helpful idea. Some people who are seen as poor, don't like being called poor. They don't see their problems or situation in those terms. They don't like being lumped together in that way.

So far people affected by all this, people who may be on low income or have little money have had little chance to say what they think. We don't often hear what people who know about these things first hand have to say. They aren't often asked. That's the aim of this project. It's to listen to what people with first hand experience of the problems included as poverty have to say.

- Give details of the project; its length, where it is based; the people who are carrying it out and supervising it and who they are.

To carry out the project, we are having discussions with a wide variety of people who have first hand experience of some of the problems associated with living on low income.

We aren't trying to find out about them – about you and your private and personal life, but what your views and ideas are about these things more generally. If you want to refer to your own experience, that's fine, but you don't have to.

Because of people's life experience, we feel that they've got a lot to offer in terms of ideas and thoughts about what the problems are and what should be done.

• Check with participants that this is clear so far.

We want to put together a book which reports what people say in their own words. We want to be sure that people we speak to have a real say in this and in what goes into the book.

To make this possible, we are asking people first if it is ok to tape record what they say in the discussion.

• Check this out to see if it is ok.

If yes:

We will send you back a transcription for you to see and make any changes you want to. Later we will send you any things you have said which we would like to include in the book in a draft so you can check them and make any changes you want and when it is produced, send you a copy of the book.

This will all be in confidence. We won't use individual names without agreement.

• Check if it is ok to use the group's name; make clear it can be anonymous.

There are some things which we'd like to discuss with you, but if there are things which we haven't thought of, or which you'd like to talk about, that's ok too. We haven't got a rigid questionnaire. You have got the final say in what we talk about.

• Check if this is clear and ok.

SCHEDULE QUESTIONS

I. THE GROUP

a) for existing group

I've met you for a discussion as a group of people who… (the focus of the group) to explore the issues that concern you.

Could you tell me a bit about the group?
What does the group do?
What are the group's objectives?
How long has the group been together?
How did you get started?
What do you think are the key issues for your group?

b) group brought together for the project

I asked you all to come together for this discussion because you are all/have in common/to hear the views of people who are… (the focus of the group) to explore the issues that concern you.

Could you tell me a bit about… (the group's common denominator)?

What are the key issues for… (people in your situation/with your experience/identity)?

What does being (their common denominator) entail?

POVERTY

I want now to talk about poverty and being poor, which is what we are focusing on in the project. As I have said, we know that some people don't think the idea of poverty is very helpful and that's one of the things we want to look at in the project. So although we are looking particularly at poverty and speaking to people from groups who might have especially helpful insights to offer, we aren't just taking the idea of poverty for granted.

2. BEING POOR

I'd like now to talk to you about your views and ideas about being poor.

What do you think it is like for people to be poor?

• Detail

What effects do you think being poor has on people?

Are there any things which you think being poor stops people doing?

What do you think are the worst things about being poor?

Do you think people treat other people differently if they are poor?

• Detail in what ways.

Does being poor make people different in any ways?

Why do you think people are poor? (Causes)

Do you think there are differences for different individuals and/or different groups?

What effect do you think it has on people to be called poor?

Do you think there are ways in which poor people as individuals and groups can try to cope with having to live on low income?

• For existing groups only:

What are the things that you do as a group which may be relevant to this?

People living on low income are often presented as if they are always reliant on other people. Are there ways in which you feel you make or have made a contribution, or helped other people?

3. HOW POVERTY IS DEFINED

I want to talk with you next about how people define poverty; what they say it means. Experts and politicians use the word a lot and have given it special meanings. I'd like to see what you think about what they say:

Offer three definitions from British Social Attitudes Survey in turn.

Would you think someone in Britain was or was not poor if:

1. They had enough to buy the things they really needed but not enough to buy the things most people take for granted.

2. They had enough to eat and live, but not enough to buy other things they needed.

3. They had not enough to eat and live without getting into debt.

• Let people see each of the statements and ask them what they think of them as a definition of poverty. Make it possible for people to express and explain any strong likes/dislikes.

Is there one definition you prefer?

How would you define the word poverty? What does poverty mean for you? (a quick brainstorming session here might be a good idea, enabling people to come up with ideas and words which they may have)

Who would you include as poor?

What would it mean for someone not to be poor?

There is a lot of talk about poverty. Do you feel poverty is a helpful term/idea/word?

Do you think there are words that describe better what people experience and the problems which are included under 'poverty'?

4. PUBLIC INTERPRETATIONS OF POVERTY

I'd like to start by asking you what you think about some of the things that are now being said about people who are on low income/disadvantaged/poor.

I'd like you to look at these and talk a bit about what you think of them.

• Selected cuttings offering a) politicians and b) media views on:

1. poverty and 'dependency'

2. 'professional' beggars and 'scroungers'

3. lone parents, delinquency and welfare queue jumping

4. the idea of the 'underclass'

Support general discussion about these cuttings, plus specific questions:

What do you think of this?

What kind of image of people do you think it gives?

What do you think of the language that is used about people?

Why do you think the media report stories on poverty?

Why do you think politicians say what they do?

5. PROPOSALS FOR ACTION ON POVERTY

I'd like to talk with you now about your thoughts and ideas for doing something about poverty. (this may include what they are already doing and/or in addition, new ideas which they have)

What do you think could be done where you live/locally/in your area to reduce disadvantage and poverty?

• If an existing group, ask if there are things the group can do.

• If not, ask if any of them are doing things.

What do you think could be done more generally, nationally in the country?

What part would you like to see people with first hand experience of living on low income play in:

a) discussions about poverty?

b) doing something about poverty/anti-poverty action?

Do you know of any examples or instances where people do this and how?

Can you think of any ways in which people with first hand experience of living on low income can be more involved in discussions and developments about poverty and disadvantage?

FINALLY

• Offer people opportunities to talk about other things which they would like to.

Are there any further issues or areas which you would like to raise which I haven't covered/mentioned?

• Detail

ENDING AND GOODBYES

Briefly restate that you will be sending them a copy of the transcription for comment and discussion. Try and get a name, address and phone number for a link person to take on this responsibility and seek agreement for a realistic turn around time for them, for example, they will send it back within two to four weeks.

Remind participants that the discussion is in confidence. Thank them for their help. Make it clear that you won't be disappearing, but that they will be hearing from you.

• Check if there are any questions.

• Check if there are any outstanding expenses. If so, as appropriate, get an invoice or receipt with a breakdown of costs.

Goodbye for now.

BIBLIOGRAPHY

UK Coalition Against Poverty, Participation Sub-Group, (1997), *Poverty And Participation: Learnings from a September 1996 workshop bringing together people living in poverty throughout the UK*, UK Coalition Against Poverty, London. 28pp
Report of a workshop held on September 18 1996, organised by the UK Coalition Against Poverty, Participation Sub-Group, bringing together people with experience of poverty from different parts of the UK. The workshop aimed both to enable and to explore the involvement of poor people. Participants broke into workshops which discussed the ways in which poor people are the same, but different; poverty in an affluent society; and combatting myths about poverty and poor people.

Hilary Russell, (Editor), (1996), *Speaking From Experience: Voices at the National Poverty Hearing*, Church Action on Poverty, Manchester, 40pp
Report of the National Poverty Hearing organised by Church Action on Poverty, held on 19 March 1996 where about 500 people came to hear what poor people who had taken part in local and regional hearings had to say. The report offers the platform contributions made by a number of people with experience of poverty at well as contributions from the floor from poor people and others including politicians, and members of voluntary organisations and also the responses of 'church leaders' and other participants.

Peter Beresford and Michael Turner, (1997), *It's Our Welfare: Report of the Citizens' Commission on the Future of the Welfare State*, London, National Institute for Social Work, ISBN 1 899942 17 3, 180pp.
Report of a two year inquiry undertaken by welfare state service users to enable welfare state service users more generally in the UK to give their views of the welfare state and their proposals for the future of welfare. The report is based on evidence from a wide range of welfare state service users, including a high proportion with experience of living on benefits and low income.

Carey Oppenheim and Lisa Harker, (1996), *Poverty The Facts: Revised and updated 3rd edition*, London, Child Poverty Action Group, ISBN 0 946744 49 1, 199pp
Provides detailed information about the scale and nature of poverty in the UK in the mid 1990s. It includes discussion of the causes, dimensions, geography, feminisation, racialisation and increasing divisions of poverty in the UK, locating these in a European context.

ATD Fourth World, ... *How to develop partnerships between* .... ondon, AT Fourth World, ISBN 0 9508514 2 0, 65pp.
Describes and draws lessons from a three year project with 110 families 'to explore the concept of partnership between very disadvantaged families and professional workers.' It shows how as people gained self-esteem and confidence, they started to see that their views might be taken seriously.

Saul .... *d care,* Harl.....
Focuses.....
security, personal social services and community .... and exclusion need to be understood as the consequences of social reactions, social and individual attitudes, policies, structures and practices which act a barriers to independence and security' to people on low income.

Local Government Anti-Poverty Unit, (1996), *Partnerships Against Poverty*, **London, Local Government Management Board, ISBN 0 7488 9481 0, 34pp.**
Based on papers presented at two workshops, addressing issues around working in partnership with voluntary and community organisations and with people experiencing poverty in the development and implementation of anti-poverty strategies and initiatives. It also includes case studies from four local authorities undertaking work in this area.

Ruth Lister and Peter Beresford, (1991), *Working Together Against Poverty: Involving poor people in action against poverty*, **London, Open Services Project and Department of Applied Social Studies, University of Bradford, ISBN 0 9517554 0 4, 23pp**
A report of a workshop bringing together people with experience of poverty and anti-poverty professionals in 1990 to discuss the involvement of poor people in anti-poverty action. It examines the obstacles to involvement and ways of involving poor people for the future.

Peter Alcock, (1997), *Understanding Poverty: Second edition*, **Basingstoke, Macmillan, ISBN 0 333 69280 2, 304pp.**
Provides a comprehensive and accessible review of research on and debates about the problem of poverty in the 1990s. It examines poverty in broader contexts, the definition and measurement of poverty, social divisions and poverty and the policy framework of poverty.